THE ROAD TO
BARCELONA

THE ROAD TO
BARCELONA

THE GLORY OF '72
AND MY LIFE IN FOOTBALL

DAVE SMITH

with Paul Smith

This edition first published in Great Britain in 2022 by

ARENA SPORT
An imprint of Birlinn Limited
West Newington House
10 Newington Road
Edinburgh
EH9 1QS

www.arenasportbooks.co.uk

ISBN: 9781913759032
eBook ISBN: 9781788853279

British Library Cataloguing-in-Publication Data
A catalogue record for this book is available on request from the British Library.

Designed and typeset by Polaris Publishing, Edinburgh
www.polarispublishing.com

Printed and bound by CPI Group (UK) Ltd, Croydon CR0 4YY

To Sheila — the light in my life then, now and always.

CONTENTS

ACKNOWLEDGEMENTS

THE ANNIVERSARY OF the triumph in Barcelona is a time for celebration and for reflection. Above all else, my eternal thanks and love go to Sheila for being by my side through the highs and the lows, for better and for worse. I've had good luck and bad, I've made good choices and I've made mistakes – the best fortune is nothing to do with football and everything to do with family and the love and support I have had. I am so incredibly proud of Sheila and our children Amanda, Melanie and Paul, as well as of Pascal, Zak and Tom (Melanie's family) and Coral, Finlay, Mia and Zara (Paul's family). To work with Paul so closely on *The Road to Barcelona* has been a privilege that few father and son partnerships get to share and I'm grateful to all who have been part of bringing this story to life, not least the team at Arena Sports for their faith in the project, and also Dave Hamilton and Ian McLean for their meticulous work in the background, as well as Colin Stein for his kind words of introduction. My thanks too go to the many who were there with me through my time in football and beyond, the men I was proud to call my team-mates. Finally, my appreciation to all in the Rangers family, including all of my good friends in the Dave

Smith Loyal Fraserburgh RSC, whose warmth and affection has never wavered in the 55 years since I first pulled on the famous blue shirt.

Dave Smith

OVER 15 YEARS as an author and across 18 books I have had the pleasure of telling some wonderful stories. In all that time, *The Road to Barcelona* remained an idea in the background, one to save for another day. Now is the right time and I'm grateful to have had the opportunity to have worked with my dad to look back over an illustrious career in football that played out, in the main, before my time. For my sisters and I, dad has always been the football hero and mum the real-life hero – both deserve to take a moment to look back at all they have achieved together with huge pride. This book would not have been possible without a team in the background, led by Hugh Andrew and Neville Moir at Birlinn and Arena Sport, supported by Peter Burns, Alan McIntosh and the photographers and image archivists whose pictures feature in the pages that follow. Special mention to Colin Macleod, a source of constant encouragement and support over many years. My appreciation also goes to the journalists and writers who went before me, many long since departed, but whose work lives on, providing such rich context around which this story has been built. The last words are reserved for Coral, Finlay, Mia and Zara for the love and the laughter, the fun and the contentment that makes every day a joy – the real dream team.

Paul Smith

FOREWORD

BY COLIN STEIN

FOOTBALL HAS ALWAYS been a game of comparisons, players held up against those that went before them and whoever followed next.

Every now and again someone comes along who breaks the mould and does things differently. I had the joy of sharing a dressing room with one of the best examples of that: Dave Smith.

It's a pleasure to introduce the story of a teammate who played such an important role in what has been such a big part of all our lives.

On the road to Barcelona in 1972, and in the European Cup Winners' Cup final against Dynamo Moscow in particular, Dave was at his very best.

I can still replay the opening goal in my mind, his raking ball cutting open the Russian defence, my touch and then the shot nestling in the back of the net. Dave laid on another with the fantastic cross for Willie Johnston's headed goal before Willie got his second to give us the cushion to see us through to that famous 3-2 win and bring a European trophy to Ibrox.

In defence and attack Dave was the conductor for us in the final, organising and cajoling everyone around him and then picking his moments to break forward and carve out opportunities when the time was right.

For anyone who saw him play regularly or lined up alongside him every week, it was no surprise that he stepped up when it mattered most. Pressure didn't seem to register with our No. 6.

He had that ability to see things that others didn't and pick opponents apart with a left foot which was as sweet as could be. I've seen him described as a Rolls Royce of a football player, and that's very fitting for a player who played the game with such elegance.

He was, in my view, a unique player.

Mind you, that didn't stop those comparisons I mentioned. From Jim Baxter to Bobby Moore, Franz Beckenbauer and many more in-between, Dave was held up in that type of company. That says a lot about what the supporters and football writers thought of him when he was in his prime – but, as you'll read in the pages which follow, he didn't want to be compared to anyone.

He thrived on doing what others wouldn't dream of – whether it was nutmegging opponents in his own box, mazy dribbles through swarms of players or arrowing balls from one corner of the pitch to the other. I can't think of anyone who did it quite the way he did.

As a forward, Dave was a dream. If you made the run, you knew that 99 times out of 100 the ball would hit you.

In other ways, a total nightmare! There's nothing that gets the heart racing faster than looking back and seeing one of your defenders weaving out of the 18-yard box as if he were playing a kick-about with his pals in the school playground. It was never any different – Old Firm fixtures and cup finals were played the same way as any other game. Underneath it all, there was a burning desire to win.

In fairness, he had the ability (and the self-belief) to play the game his way. He'd be the first to tell you we had nothing to worry about!

That confidence on the pitch was a hallmark of a player who is a true Rangers great, immaculate in everything he did.

That swagger was left at the tunnel entrance, though. Off the pitch he's a down-to-earth character. Those who don't know Dave might say he's shy – those of us who do would tell a different story. Once he's comfortable in your company that's when you really get to know him.

Dave was a big character in our squad, one of the leaders in the group on and off the park. That came to the fore in '72 in some style.

I hope you enjoy reading about his life in football as much as I did being part of it.

INTRODUCTION

'JUST ANOTHER GAME'

JUST ANOTHER GAME. It's a phrase I've used so many times to describe those 90 minutes in the Nou Camp and the big matches on the road to Barcelona.

For me, no match was any different. Right back to my first steps in the game through to European finals in my prime and then the final throes of a long career, the only pressure I felt was from within.

To be the best, to take a chance, to be different, to do the unexpected, to entertain.

Everything on the outside – managers on the sidelines, the opposition, the expectation of supporters, media interest – didn't really matter. To talk about pressure and football in the same breath just doesn't make sense. It was a pleasure. If I could go back in time and do it all over again I would in a heartbeat.

In that sense, when we crossed the white line to face Dynamo Moscow at the Nou Camp on 24 May 1972, it was just another game.

The truth for all of us who came back into the dressing room as European Cup Winners' Cup winners that night is that it wasn't just another game. It changed our lives forever.

Ninety minutes that have touched everything that has followed. We know now that it was a huge moment in time. We didn't know it then, and I haven't ever really acknowledged it since.

Fifty years on, it feels like the right time to reflect properly and to replay that period while it's still vivid in the mind.

What follows isn't a football autobiography in the traditional sense. For one, I don't think you want to know the ins and outs of my table tennis triumphs as a young boy or about my retirement in the glens. More importantly, there are parts of my life that I will forever keep private. For that I make no apologies.

The Road to Barcelona brings together my recollections around the glory of '72, the foundations it was built on and the experiences in the aftermath.

For those who were there or who joined the party when we arrived back in Glasgow, I hope I can do justice to the memories we share.

For those too young to have experienced it first hand, you'll have to trust that we really did have the privilege of living through the best of times.

The fact that half a century on we hold the honour of being the only Rangers team to have brought continental silverware back to Ibrox is something that not one of us would have predicted.

I was one of those who had suffered the pain of defeat against Bayern Munich in the final of the same competition five years earlier, and to lay that to rest in Barcelona was an incredible feeling.

When we stepped off the plane on home soil with the trophy in hand, we felt ready to take on the world. Never mind waiting decades, we believed we could and would go on to win on that big stage again the next year and for years after that. You feel invincible.

The history books tell a different tale, and who knows when that time will come again. I've seen a lot over the years, the domestic dominance and glimmers of hope in Europe. I've sat in the stands during the darkest of days and been there for the revival, at home and abroad. I've felt the pain and shared the hope. Like everyone with Rangers in their heart, I'll never say never.

Until then, the memories of '72 carry through the generations. It's a story worth telling.

ONE

'BARCELONA BELONGED TO RANGERS'

EIGHT YEARS ON the Rangers playing staff, more than 300 competitive games, incredible highs, painful lows – and it all came down to one night in Barcelona.

When we boarded the plane to set off for Spain, it was a huge relief. All the waiting and all the hype were left behind at the departure gate. It was our time.

And what a time it was!

T-Rex, Elton John, The Drifters and the Rolling Stones were in the top 10, and Led Zeppelin were heading for Green's Playhouse to entertain an appreciative Glasgow crowd.

Diamonds are Forever and *The Godfather* were breaking all sorts of box-office records at the cinema, and *Emmerdale Farm* and *Are You Being Served?* made their TV debuts. French Connection was making waves as the new brand on the fashion scene, and the Ford Cortina was flying off the forecourt as the UK's bestseller.

In sport, the Olympic torch was wending its way to Munich for the summer games, and Lee Trevino was heading for Muirfield to defend his Open title. Brian Clough led Derby County to the English championship, collecting his first trophy as a manager. What would become of him?

The average house price in Scotland was £7,000, and the suburbs were beginning to sprawl as the likes of John Lawrence and Wimpey continued to cater for the masses. In the city, the skyline was changing as the tower blocks continued to rise from the ground.

It wasn't all good times, far from it. The Upper Clyde Shipbuilders protests were in full swing as the spectre of yard closures and thousands of redundancies loomed amid massive political unrest. The year had started with the miners' strike – and by February power shortages were leading to restrictions and managed power cuts as the authorities tried to keep the lights on across the UK.

I would love to say I remember all of that and it's ingrained in my memory in glorious technicolour.

The truth? As a player, you're so wrapped up in your own wonderful little bubble that very little on the outside gets through.

Music, films, TV, cars – that wasn't me. Football was what my life revolved around, and the week that lay ahead was huge. It would end either with a winner's medal to mark my Ibrox career or leave me still searching for silverware.

From a personal perspective, the clock was ticking, and I knew that. I was six months away from my 29th birthday and it was an era in which 30 was considered an old man in football terms. I'd been at the club for six years and had nothing to show for it through a combination of bad luck and more bad luck. This was the chance to put all that right in one game.

All things considered, you'd think tensions would be running high – but nothing could have been further from the truth. As a group we were in great spirits. I don't think there was a single player who climbed the stairs to that plane who had any doubt that we were bringing home the cup. The doubt maybe crept in 80 minutes into the match for some ... but that's for another chapter.

That confidence came from the talent we had and the belief there was in what we had set out to achieve in Europe when the adventure had begun eight months earlier.

It's fair to say it didn't come from a sparkling season on Scottish soil, and that, if anything, makes the success of '72 all the more remarkable.

In the league we had finished third, short of top spot by a long stretch and six points behind Aberdeen in second place after an indifferent end to the season. Once the championship had gone, results understandably tailed off – playing for a runners-up medal is never the biggest incentive. Of course, you want to win every game, but the edge is gone as soon as the big prize is out of reach.

I was once fined by the football authorities for declining the honour of picking up a Highland League Cup runners-up medal as player-manager at Peterhead in the early 1980s, on the back of a refereeing performance that left a lot to be desired. You might call it sour grapes, the association certainly saw it as disrespectful. You could argue both, but being a good loser isn't a quality I've ever claimed to have.

The problem we had at Rangers at that time was we had been second too many times and we were desperate to put it right for the supporters as much as for ourselves. I can't begin to explain how much it meant to do that in Europe.

I'd arrived from Aberdeen in 1966, and the aim was to wrest the league trophy back from the other side of the city. In that first season we were three points short after three draws in the last three games of the campaign. The next year we lost out by two points after a draw and a defeat in the final three games, our only loss in the league that term.

And so it went on. The league table might have told a different story at times, but we never felt there was a big gap. As a squad we didn't feel inferior, but nobody remembers the team which comes second.

It was a difficult time to be connected with the club, and we needed to put smiles back on faces.

Derek Johnstone had done that 18 months earlier with his winner against Celtic in the 1970 League Cup final, something everyone hoped would be a springboard to better times and was probably the point the tide began to turn. I missed that final with one of two broken legs I suffered in that period (see my earlier note about bad luck).

That was Willie Waddell's first trophy as Rangers manager and was a case of laying down a marker.

Waddell is a figure who features prominently in the pages which follow and a character so integral to Rangers as a player, manager and administrator. It feels wrong not to be calling him Mr Waddell, even now, but maybe it's time to lay that deference to one side.

He was one of four managers I served under in a blue shirt, and all had their own attributes. In the case of Waddell, it was a knack for making the right calls at the right time.

He arrived late in 1969 when the only way was up, and he left the manager's office on his own terms in the summer of '72. His signings paid off, his team selections and tactical changes more often than not worked out. You could call it good fortune or managerial nous, but whatever it was it worked in our favour.

We had our moments – as you'll begin to understand, I wasn't the easiest to coach – but there was a mutual respect. He had a presence and the confidence you need to be a Rangers manager, built on his reputation as a player. Not that any of us were in awe of a legend returning, but we knew he was a man of substance.

Waddell had replaced Davie White. The circumstances are well told, but worth repeating. Having led Kilmarnock to the league title, Waddell had made the astute decision to step aside while the going was good and went from gamekeeper to poacher as a football writer. He was critical of White – the Boy David as he had called him in print – and eventually the pressure from all sides told. The decision was made, and it was out with the new, in the shape of White, and in with the old, in Waddell.

I'd watched him from the terraces as a boy and remembered him as a powerful winger, fast and direct. He'd lost none of that presence when he swapped playing kit for a suit, heavier than his playing weight and cutting an imposing figure.

In later years I watched from the outside as he made his mark as a manager at Kilmarnock. What he achieved at Rugby Park, winning the championship in 1965, was remarkable, and when we talk of the great Scottish managers I think he's all too often overlooked. With Killie and then Rangers he did things which are unlikely ever to be repeated.

I also got to know Waddell as a football writer, one of the inner circle of Scottish pressmen. The relationships between that press corps and players were sacrosanct – we trusted them implicitly, knowing that anything we told them privately would stay that way. We regarded them as friends.

Waddell was one of the callers to the room John Greig and I shared in Poland, when we travelled out to play Gornik Zabrze in the European Cup Winners' Cup in November 1969 and fell to a 3-1 defeat in the game that sounded the death knell for White's time in charge. He came to pick the bones of that game and that result over a post-match drink. If he knew at that stage he would soon be swapping the press box for the dugout he never let on to us.

But that's exactly what transpired. White was shown the door, and the red carpet was rolled out for Waddell. It was quite the comeback for a seemingly retired manager, although he was only 48 when he took on the job at Ibrox.

It was an interesting change of direction for the board, who had gone with White as a nod to the changing of the guard in Scottish football. Coaching was evolving, and the directors had been looking at what was happening elsewhere – Eddie Turnbull at Aberdeen, Jock Stein at Celtic – and wanted to make that transition. The age of the tracksuit manager was upon us.

White was in that image, a coach rather than a traditional manager.

That was night and day to Scot Symon, the man who had brought me to the club.

We didn't see a lot of Symon day to day. He would appear occasionally, dapper in his suit and bowler hat, but his role was far less hands-on than those who followed him. He made the signings and picked the team – although the side practically picked itself. There was no rotation. It was the best 11 week to week, and I'm a great believer that's the way every player would want it. That was the case in the 1960s just as it is in the 2020s. You don't feel tired when you pull your boots on and run out of that tunnel.

Symon was a true gentleman and, quite rightly, a Rangers legend. He could have been treated better by the club, and it was painful to see it end the way it did for him when he was relieved of his duties in November 1967. We all liked and respected him, and as a player you always feel a responsibility when a manager loses their job, particularly one you admire and feel indebted to. He'd given me my dream opportunity, and I'll forever owe him for that.

The sacking was as much of a surprise to the players as it was to the manager. John Greig and I were at the TV studios in Clydebank to record *Quiz Ball* (think *University Challenge* crossed with *Question of Sport* and you'll not be far away), with the inimitable Rikki Fulton as our guest supporter. The manager, who was leading the quiz team, had run us there and back to Queen Street station at the end of the show. He was in good spirits, and there was no indication anything was afoot. The next morning, he was gone.

In case you're wondering, we lost the quiz 3-1 to Tottenham Hotspur, and by the time it was broadcast they had the awkward situation of having the former Rangers manager as one of the team captains.

With White, we had more of an inkling that it was not going to end well. The mood music wasn't good, and the negativity was growing.

White didn't have the authority or the aura of the Rangers managers who went before him or who followed after. He didn't have the media presence or the stature. That wasn't something he could change – he had the football brain, there's no doubt about it, and I genuinely believe he could have gone on to have success at Ibrox. It was a brave appointment – but the board didn't have the confidence to see through the project, understandably spooked by results and the signs they were seeing.

If there was a criticism of White I would say it was that he perhaps didn't understand the enormity of the job he had or the responsibility that went with it. I've no doubt that dawned on him further down the line. We would all love the benefit of hindsight after all.

He allowed himself to get too close to the players. He wanted to be one of the boys. I'll always remember one trip overseas, watching him finishing his meal on the table with the directors and being first on the dance floor. No big deal, but not what you traditionally see from a Rangers manager!

Safe to say, he wasn't a disciplinarian like those before and after him.

We were used to having to creep back to our rooms if we'd stayed out for a nightcap later than we should have done when we were on tour. With White, we got an invitation to carry on through the night and go straight to training rather than being packed off to bed. I can remember the directors watching one of those drills, not knowing we were more than a little the worse for wear and no doubt wondering why on earth we weren't exactly setting the heather alight as we fired crosses at

Alex Ferguson, standing forlorn in the penalty box, and not a single one landed.

If White seemed to be a fish out of water, Waddell was made for the job. He looked the part and spoke a good game. The directors had turned to the Ibrox establishment, and it paid off in great style, not just with the cups he won but with the foundations he laid and the team he assembled on and off the park.

Waddell had the stubborn streak that you need as a Rangers manager, knowing that he could afford to be so because of the power that goes with having your name over the door.

When you ventured up the marble staircase at Ibrox to the manager's office, with him sitting behind the big old wooden desk with his glasses propped on the end of his nose, you invariably knew the answer to whatever question you were about to ask. Usually, it was an emphatic no.

Not long after he arrived as manager, the players held a meeting downstairs to discuss joining the players' union. It was a movement which was just starting out, the infancy of PFA Scotland as it is now, and it made perfect sense for players to try and establish that collective voice. The decision was made – the Ibrox squad wanted in, the players had spoken.

John and I bounded up the stairs to pass on the good news to the manager, pressed the buzzer outside and waited for the light to glow to allow us in. You never entered when the red light was showing, you always had to get permission.

In we went and told him the decision the players had made. He peered over his glasses and quite calmly said: 'You'll no be joining any union.' Matter closed, end of story. So much for player power.

After I broke my leg for the second time I made another trip up the stairs, pressed the buzzer and waited to be summoned in. Up to my knee in plaster and on crutches, I was there to ask for a couple of complimentary tickets for the next game. He looked me up and down and asked, 'Are you playing at the weekend?'

'Do I look like I'm playing?'

'Well, you know the rules – there are only tickets if you're in the squad.'

And off I hobbled.

Ten minutes later the doorman, Bobby Moffat, came and found me. He went to hand me two tickets courtesy of 'the Boss' as Bobby called him. I told him to go and tell 'the Boss' to stick the tickets wherever he liked. I don't think that message got passed on – Bobby was a bit more diplomatic than I ever was!

That was the way Waddell was. He liked everyone to know who was in charge, and I respected that. It helped that he liked me as a player too. He had always given me good reviews in the papers and one of the first things he did was put me back in the team after the failed experiment bringing Jim Baxter back under White.

He was ruthless in that sense. It didn't matter if you were idolised on the terraces. Baxter went out the door, Willie Henderson was allowed to move on before the European final, and Willie Johnston and Colin Stein likewise after Barcelona. Brave decisions, although not the right one in the case of Bud and Steiny who in time were brought back.

In his first full season, Waddell took the League Cup back to Ibrox, and in his second it was the European Cup Winners' Cup that was within reach as the summer of '72 loomed – even if circumstances conspired to make it not the smoothest build-up to the final.

From playing our last league match, a 4-2 win at home to Ayr United on 1 May, to lining up against Dynamo Moscow, we had a three-week lull. As preparation for the biggest game of our lives, it was far from ideal.

Bizarrely, there was talk of us flying out to Indonesia to play an exhibition match against their national side. It would have been an odd time to be trekking across the world to play in tropical conditions, but you learnt to expect the unexpected. That one never did come to fruition, and I don't think our preparation for the cup final suffered for not taking on that particular challenge.

The solution was to slot in a couple of bounce games, although the choice of opponents raised a few eyebrows in our own camp and I'm sure it did on the outside too.

The might of an Inverness Select, drawn from the Highland League, were our first opponents. A Wednesday night encounter at Grant Street Park, home of Clachnacuddin – just the thing to get the pulse racing! It wasn't quite the Nou Camp in terms of scale or climate.

It was a testimonial match for Ally Chisholm, Ernie Latham and Chic Allan. It was the first time a Rangers side had been in Inverness for 20 years, and the hope was that it would draw a big crowd to keep us on our toes. In the end it pulled in more than 7,000 supporters, so it served its purpose.

Andy Penman, more naturally considered a winger, was played in the middle of the park that night as the manager tinkered a little with the approach and looked at his options for our trip to Barcelona.

My hunch would be that he wanted to find a way to include Andy, who had bags of experience and never let us down when he played. His other options were more youthful, with Derek Parlane and Alfie Conn also in the running, and maybe he was leaning towards an older head on such a big occasion.

Derek was also one of a number trying to prove they were physically ready for Barcelona, after suffering a knock in the weeks leading up to the final.

At the end of a long season there were plenty of bumps, bruises and worse to contend with. Colin Jackson's fitness was a worry after he had picked up a knee injury, and John Greig's ankle knock was the other major concern. John made the trip to the Highlands and played away fine in a cameo from the bench. Colin had to sit it out.

He was probably the biggest injury worry, the one with the question mark over his head. He'd suffered ligament damage in the final weeks of the season, and it's impossible with an injury like that to know how it is going to react. It can feel fine in fitness tests and the like, and then one twist or turn knocks it back a week or two. The clock was ticking.

That game at Inverness was a fortnight before the match in Barcelona, and it was a case of fine-tuning the squad.

The highest-profile omission from that list was not due to injury, it was down to the hard-line approach which typified Waddell as the man making those big calls.

Willie Henderson, so often a talisman for Rangers, would be watching from afar. His departure had been confirmed as the rest of us were preparing for the trip to Spain, one of the names on a list of players released. It was a low-key end to a career which had been anything but.

On the outside, I think there was surprise at the decision to let him go. The club had a three-year option on his contract, and he was a player known across the world. Inside, I don't think any of us saw a different outcome once he and the manager had locked horns.

It was the end of a turbulent period. After being dropped into the reserves, he walked out and said he wouldn't be back. When he did return, the manager suspended him for a month. They weren't on each other's Christmas card list it's fair to say.

Willie quickly took up an offer to go out to South Africa with Durban City while he considered his options, during the same period we were packing our bags for Barcelona.

You might think it would have been a distraction for us, but in reality it has never been a business with much room for sentiment. Players come, players go. For those who remain it's a case of on to the next challenge.

In our case that lay in the Highlands. We won the game in Inverness 5-2 and had a matching result six days later when we played St Mirren in the second and last of the warm-up games.

That was at Love Street – with an Alfie Conn hat-trick stealing the show. Would that have any bearing on the team selection in Spain? Maybe, just maybe.

A clutch of us played both of those games – myself, Sandy Jardine, Alex Macdonald, John Greig from the bench, Andy Penman, Colin Stein, Willie Johnston, Derek Johnstone and Derek Parlane. Another nod to the fact the manager was giving Andy and Derek a chance to play their way in, or was he indulging in a bit of kidology with the Russian scouts looking in from afar?

Tommy McLean had been sent home from training before the St Mirren game, suffering from a throat infection, and it was those little uncontrollable things that perhaps posed the biggest risk to the preparations. Something like that could easily have taken out half of the team if they hadn't acted quickly.

With the manager out in Russia to watch Dynamo in a league match against Kairat, it was Willie Thornton in charge of us back in Paisley. Thornton was a real gent and a calming influence around the squad. I think Waddell appreciated his good counsel behind the scenes too.

St Mirren had apparently been asked to give us a tough test, although they took that brief to extremes with some of the tackles that were flying in. You got used to that as a Rangers player, but a few days before a European final wasn't the time to be picking battles on the pitch.

In-between, we trained pretty much as normal, kept ticking over by the coaching staff. We should have been grateful for the recuperation time after a long season – we had played 59 competitive games up to that point – but as a player you don't want to stop once you're into that rhythm.

Match sharpness is so different from fitness. Yes, we could keep ourselves in shape during that extended downtime, but staying tuned in was far more difficult.

The two friendlies served a purpose, but with nothing at stake it's a very different proposition to playing in competitive fixtures. With the season over for everyone else, there also wasn't a queue of opposition teams lining up for extra games. Most teams were demob happy, and the fact we had any games at all was fortunate.

While we were at home trying to stay in shape, the manager had completed his trip to Russia to see the opposition in the flesh and had touched down in Spain to make a final check on our base out there. It was typical of his attention to detail and the desire to be in control of every facet.

Finding out about the opposition we were about to face wasn't a simple task, not like in previous ties against the likes of Bayern Munich of Germany and Torino of Italy.

It's easy to forget that European football was still in its infancy really, particularly for some of the club sides we found ourselves competing against during my time at Rangers and certainly for Dynamo.

Soviet teams had joined as part of the expansion of the UEFA competitions and had only five or six years under their belts by the time the men from Moscow made it to Barcelona in 1972. They had the distinction of becoming the first team from what was then the USSR to reach a final, but it was another three years until there was a winner, with Dynamo Kiev beating Hungarian opposition in the form of Ferencvaros.

Dinamo Tbilisi went on to beat German side Carl Zeiss Jena in 1981, and Dynamo Kiev beat Atletico Madrid in the 1986 final to complete a hat-trick.

Dynamo Moscow, in our era, were the big hitters along with their city rivals Spartak. There was always said to be a connection with the secret police, stretching back long before we played them.

There was also a story behind the blue-and-white kit, which could be traced back to their formation under Harry Charnock. As the name suggests, it was an Englishman rather than a Muscovite who set up the club, and as a Blackburn Rovers supporter he went for colours which reminded him of home.

He and his brothers had moved out to work in the cotton industry with their father and launched a works team that went on to become a giant of the game in their adopted country. Apparently, the idea was to persuade the factory staff to refrain from drinking vodka and play football instead, and so the Orekhovo Sports Club was born. It sounds like a plan that couldn't possibly fail.

They fled the country in 1919 after the Russian Revolution, and the team, which had enjoyed plenty of success, was taken over by the head of the Cheka – the country's first secret police force, before the KGB – and renamed Dynamo Moscow.

And there ends the history lesson!

They went on to win a string of league titles, particularly in the early days, and were still a force to be reckoned with in the 1950s, 1960s and 1970s. They've yet to reach another European final though.

Then, and now, their biggest claim to fame is as the home to Lev Yashin. He was the poster boy of Russian football, spending his entire playing career with Dynamo, all 20 years of it, and is still the only goalkeeper ever to win the Ballon d'Or. We saw very little of him playing for his club, other than the rare forays to Britain for exhibition games, but everyone was aware of the legend that was Yashin from his World Cup and international exploits. He was a goalkeeper who did things with style.

Thankfully, by '72 he had packed away his gloves and was confined to the sidelines, still attached to the club and part of the backroom team for the final. Even though he wasn't going to be on the park, he gave Dynamo star quality and was the main focus of media attention when it came to Moscow.

As for the team we were going to face, they were largely unknown in the West – but we could rely on Waddell to keep us right.

Even when he had to go behind the Iron Curtain, he was able to furnish us with the usual pen pictures and every bit of information you could ever want on the opposition. No stone was left unturned, there was never any room left for excuses.

Waddell had dedicated himself to the coaching profession. He had travelled to Italy in the early 1960s to study the methods of Internazionale's Helenio Herrera, an Argentine master of his craft who won the European Cup twice with Inter. Legend has it that he slept next to a model of a football pitch, and it wouldn't surprise me if Waddell kept a tactics board on his bedside table too.

By the time we set off for Barcelona it was pretty much over to us as players. The manager's preparation had been done long before we arrived.

The departure was all part of the big build-up, with the official Rangers party piped onto the plane and given a formal send-off by Glasgow's Lord Provost John Mains.

The hype had been building through the week. I even had photographers out at the house to get shots of me packing my boots for the trip.

We flew out from Prestwick on the Sunday, travelling down from Ibrox by coach. You had players parking at the ground, some being dropped at the door and others walking up from the subway to gather together with bags in hand like an excitable class gathering for a school trip.

Our wives were part of the travelling contingent but flew out separately and were whisked away to stay in Sitges courtesy of the club while we headed for our base at Castelldefels, south of the city on the Costa del Garraf. The Gran Hotel Rey Don Jaime was to be home for the days ahead, perched on a hillside and away from prying eyes.

It was a quiet coastal hideaway in those days, and suited us perfectly. Since then, it has quadrupled in size – not quite the sleepy hollow it once was and there's a bit more of a sprinkling of stardust. Now it is home to the likes of Lionel Messi. It's good to know that he's chosen to follow in the footsteps of football legends.

We travelled with a big squad, for that era at least. The back-up goalkeepers Bobby Watson and Gerry Neef were included as cover for Peter McCloy, and there were plenty of outfield options, which proved to be important.

There was a sense of kid gloves around us once we reached Castelldefels. We wore tracksuits rather than shorts by the pool, to guard against sunburn, and we took our own provisions with us, as we had done frequently on European trips, in a nod to the manager's fears about stomach upsets. A hamper full of Aberdeen Angus wasn't unusual in the hold of our charter planes – high steaks, you might say! Without giving too much away, I'm afraid the jokes don't get much better.

From the moment we landed in Barcelona we got a sense of how big a support had made the journey. It felt like there were Rangers fans around every corner. The airport was a sea of red, white and blue. Hats, scarfs, jackets, kilts and even berets. You name it, the colours were everywhere, and Barcelona belonged to Rangers.

TWO

'YOU COULD DARE TO DREAM'

THAT FLIGHT TO Barcelona was the end of a far longer journey for me. From the muddy playing fields of Aberdeen to the hallowed turf of the Nou Camp, there had been a few bends in the road to navigate.

Every one of us had followed our own path, and to get under the skin of '72 you have to rewind further back, back to where it all began.

From 1 to 11 we came from different cities and towns, with different backgrounds and different stories. The one thing in common was the love of football which started as soon as we could kick a ball. No TV cameras, no crowds – just the adrenaline rush of beating a man or scoring a goal. We didn't know it then, but that is what we'd spend our lives chasing and the same thing that drove us on every time the going got tough on that run to Barcelona.

For me football was in the blood. A bit of a cliché? Maybe, but I think the Smiths have as genuine a claim to that as anyone.

My dad, Jimmy, was an all-round sportsman, an excellent tennis player and no stranger to the football field. He played junior football with Woodside and was part of the team from

Aberdeen that won the Newlands Cup, run by the National Dock Labour Board and contested by harbour works teams from across Britain.

On my mum Margaret's side, my two uncles were good players at a decent level. Alex Baigrie started out at Aberdeen and played with Forres Mechanics in the Highland League. Hugh Baigrie also cut his teeth in the juniors in Aberdeen, another Woodside player in the family, before being tempted south by Partick Thistle in the pre-war days. He also turned out for Ayr and Montrose and based himself in Glasgow after he hung up his boots. I would stay with him in Springhill after I made the move to Rangers, while I was still commuting from the North-east.

My cousin Hughie Hay, another on my mum's side, was probably the most notable of the elder footballing statesmen in the family and the one I remember playing, just 12 years my senior. He progressed from Banks o' Dee in junior football to Aberdeen early in the 1950s and was destined for great things before a leg break during his national service got in the way. It meant he missed the Dons' title-winning season in 1954/55 and he never properly got going after that, playing out his career with Dundee United and Arbroath. It was a formidable Aberdeen team at that time, winning the league and cups, and I remember being part of some huge crowds at Pittodrie as a young boy.

The game ran through to the next generation.

My brother Doug, six years my senior, was the first to shine. Doug grew to become what I would describe as the perfect centre-half – good in the air, a brilliant reader of the game, sharp in the tackle and a very intelligent user of the ball.

He came through the ranks at Aberdeen Lads' Club and, after serving his time training to become a painter and decorator, was tempted down the road and miles by Dundee United in 1959 with the promise of senior football, learning the football trade alongside fellow Lads' Club protégé Ron Yeats at Tannadice. Ronnie went on to become the first Liverpool captain to lift the FA Cup, and it was his move to Anfield that opened the door for Doug to establish himself.

When Doug made that move in the late 1950s, I don't think anyone in the family expected that association would last a lifetime. When he eventually retired from playing in 1976, he had played 628 competitive games, risen to become club captain and was the rock which the club had been rebuilt around – in an era in which they beat Barcelona home and away as well as reaching United's first ever Scottish Cup final. There was a ten-year spell in which he missed just four games, a model of consistency and a leader of men.

After his playing days, Doug – who was successful in the pub trade in Dundee as mine host at the Athletic Bar – joined the board at Tannadice in the early 1980s and gave sterling service as a director, vice-chairman and, following Jim McLean's departure, chairman. He served the Scottish Football Association and the Scottish Football League too in various offices, including President of the SFL, and was one of the most influential figures in the Scottish game.

His passing in 2012, at the age of 75, brought tributes from across the football community and underlined the respect there was for him. Doug was a wonderful football player, the best all-round in the family and I would say of his generation in that position in Scotland, but above all else he was a gentleman. When life is flying along you don't really take the time to say all the things you wish you had. I hope Doug knew how much I admired him – how much I wish I could have been more like him. It is a word overused in football, but he was my hero.

While Doug was making his way in football, so too was our brother Hugh. Five years older than me, he followed in Doug's bootsteps, albeit a very different player.

He was what I'd describe as a mercurial winger – a nightmare for opposition full-backs, who didn't know where he was going to turn next. (I'm not sure he always did either!) I couldn't begin to tell you how many defenders got sent off or booked trying to get the ball from him. He was impossible to pin down.

He had pace and strength into the bargain, a daunting package as an attacking player.

Hughie's talent shone for everyone to see, and he was part of the Aberdeen school select alongside Denis Law as they went on to win the Scottish Primary Schools Cup in 1951. Mind you, Denis only made the bench that day.

A Scottish schoolboys' cap followed, and Hughie had a good career in the senior game with Forfar Athletic and Morton, where he helped them up to the old First Division, as well as turning out in the Highland League with Forres Mechanics. He had a choice to make between full-time football and putting his energy into his career outside of the game. He chose the latter, which was absolutely the right choice for him.

Hughie was as bright in the classroom as he was on the football pitch and won a scholarship to Robert Gordon's College in the city. He made the best of that private education and had a very successful career in accountancy – for all he may have admired some of my achievements in football, he probably never knew how proud I was of his career and what he accomplished. Hugh passed away in 2017 at the age of 79 and will be remembered most as a man who would do anything for anyone.

For a working-class lad, he proved that there's no ceiling if you're prepared to work hard. We all had that same determination to succeed in whatever we did.

My dad was a docker with the Aberdeen Harbour Board when we were growing up, and we moved from the Gallowgate in the city centre up to a new council estate to the north of the city as they sprung up in the post-war years. We were the first residents of the prefab houses built at Provost Rust Drive, designed as a temporary solution to the housing shortages of the time. They're still standing now, more than 70 years on, and at what was our house there's still a wonky gate post that I hit when I overshot one of my first parking attempts after passing my test. My driving hasn't improved too much over the years.

Northfield and Middlefield, where I grew up, are among Aberdeen's areas of 'deprivation' today, according to government measures. To me it's wrong to talk of deprived areas, whether now or then. The Smith boys were well looked after and loved in a hard-working family and were incredibly wealthy in terms of the opportunities we had to play and grow in an environment which taught us so much about life.

The lesson at home and at school – I went to Middlefield Primary and then on to Hilton Secondary – was that you could dare to dream.

In primary school we had a Polish PE teacher and would call at his house on the way to school games, desperate to get to the pitch and get started. He just let us play, it was perfect. Or he did most of the time.

I remember pleading with him to let me stay on in a school game at the Harlaw pitches in Aberdeen. We were winning 6-0 and I'd scored five by then. He said he was taking me off to even up the game. I explained I was on a penny a goal up to six, and then it went up to sixpence after that. He cost me a small fortune that day by substituting me!

By the time I moved up to secondary school I was assured of a place in the team because Doug had gone before me. He was the best player in the school, and it meant I walked into the side.

I think when you're immersed in the game like that from such an early age it makes the extraordinary feel ordinary. A career in football was still a dream, like every kid who pulls on a pair of boots, but it was one that I knew was in reach.

Don't get me wrong, it didn't mean I didn't have to work at it.

As well as playing with my school team I turned out for Lads' Club, just as Doug, Ronnie Yeats, Denis Law, Jocky Scott and many others before and after did.

When you look back, it was a golden era for football in the city, a stream of players coming through. Aside from those I mentioned from Lads' Club, there was also Martin Buchan, who went on to captain Aberdeen and earn his big move to Manchester United.

Why there were so many good players in that period is difficult to say, there's certainly never been a period like it since. Simply put, I'd say it was because we had nothing else to distract us – football was our life from such a young age, and we played morning, noon and night. The debate now about how many touches young players need, coming through the performance schools and academies, is an interesting one. If you added up the touches we had it would be far greater than anything that can be replicated in a formal structure.

Being a Lads' Club boy was more than just playing for a team – there were two youth clubs, where you could play football and other sports after school and at weekends. Table tennis was my other big love then – the hours spent on the tables in Aberdeen as a boy served me well when we had competitions at Ibrox, where there was a table under the stands. My dad was a great player too.

Even after I turned professional with Aberdeen, I'd go along to the Lads' Club on a Saturday night to play three-a-side football games long into the night. I didn't tell the club, of course; I doubt they would have encouraged one of their prized assets to be running around a games hall and dodging tackles.

I suppose that goes to show that I didn't really see football as a job. It was always a game for me. It isn't like choosing a career in engineering or construction – it chooses you from a pretty young age.

There had been interest from further afield than Aberdeen. Reuben Bennett, heralded as the founder of the boot-room coaching tradition at Liverpool, was sent north from Anfield to try and tempt me down to England as a teenager.

Bennett had been a goalkeeper in the Scottish leagues and manager at Ayr United, but it was under Bill Shankly that he flourished as a coach. It wasn't surprising they kept a close eye on what was happening back on home soil. The likes of Ian St John and Ronnie Yeats had been signed as senior players, and they also kept tabs on the youth scene.

They'd been tipped off about a skinny young boy who was training with Aberdeen and after watching me they made the offer to join. Bennett came to the house and spoke to my mum to try and persuade me, but I wasn't keen. I was a home-bird if the truth be told.

It wasn't until I was 17, in 1961, that the Aberdeen move became official. Plenty others younger than me had been signed, taken in as groundstaff as was the way for those who were considered to be the best players in those days, long before the advent of S-forms or youth academies. In that sense I was a late starter.

By then I had already started my apprenticeship as a draughtsman in a drawing office in the middle of the city, combining that with college. What I don't know about structural steel isn't worth knowing. Or is it that what I *do* know about structural steel isn't worth knowing? I'll let you be the judge!

Once I signed for Aberdeen it became more and more difficult to combine work and football. I'd be doing hard shifts on the training field and then having to sit through hours of night classes, and in the end I decided to concentrate my efforts on giving everything I had to make it at Pittodrie.

After getting my foot in the door, I didn't look back. I went into the first team early – I was 18 when I made my debut against St Johnstone in January 1962.

An injury had paved the way for me to play in that game, and I never really looked back. At that age you take it all in your stride, you don't really soak in the experiences which are coming at you thick and fast. First game, first goal ... I'd love to say I remembered them all, but you don't stop to look around.

By then I'd come through the reserves and, despite a distinct lack of bulk, had proved I could play as a boy among men. I weighed about 10 stone when I started playing, and no amount of Sweetheart Stout and steak – the go-to for building people up in the days before protein shakes – was going to turn me into a muscleman.

What I lacked in physique I made up for in guile and confidence. The reserve league was a great character-building experience, a chance for the youngster to play with and against the more worldly wise. It tended to be veterans playing out their time, or those coming back from injury, so there was a good mix.

But it was once you moved into the first team that the real education came.

It was Rangers icon Bobby Shearer who gave me my introduction to the big bad world of Scottish football, and it came at Ibrox, playing for Aberdeen. I faced up to him and popped the ball through his legs. He caught up with me after and said, 'Son, don't do that again.' The next time I got the ball I couldn't resist it – back through the legs and away. All I remember after that is lying on the ground with Bobby towering over me, having kneed my thigh and left me flat out. I was waiting to get another blast, but he said, 'Son, are you okay?' That was Bobby, a fearless competitor but a good man. I didn't have the privilege of playing with him at Ibrox, but we did bump into each other, in a less painful way, over the years and I always enjoyed his company.

That set the tone for what was to come. I never got intimidated on the park, whoever I was facing. That type of attitude I think was what earned me my break at a time when Aberdeen were crying out for fresh blood.

From that first game in 1962 through to when I left for Rangers in the summer of 1966 I played 166 competitive games and won my first Scotland cap. I'll forever be grateful for the chance the club gave me.

THREE

'NOTHING WORTH HAVING COMES EASILY'

I WAS YOUNG and impatient, I can see that now. It felt like there were too many players at Aberdeen who were in a comfort zone, happy to pick up their wages and content with mid-table. I wanted to be in a side that was challenging, not just drifting along.

The reality was it was a selling club. Someone had to go just about every summer to balance the books. George Kinnell went to Stoke City for £35,000, Doug Fraser to West Brom for £23,000 and Charlie Cooke to Dundee for £40,000. They were all substantial fees, and it was a model that served Aberdeen well. I had it my mind from early on that I would be next. If they had been able to keep us all together it would have been a very competitive side, but that wasn't part of the business plan at the time.

Even in the heyday under Alex Ferguson they had to wheel and deal, aiming to sell big to reinvest in the core group. That was something Dundee United did very well too, during my brother Doug's time on the board, and it should be the model for every provincial club.

The flip side of that sell-big approach from my time at Aberdeen was a clutch of local boys who sat in the reserves for years, never getting near the first team. There was a whole squad in their early 20s, far from young kids, who spent a long time just treading water. It was as though Aberdeen were too nice to let them go, they felt obliged to keep them on the staff.

Nice would be a good word to describe the club, and I don't mean that as a slight. It had a real family feel – the city can be a bit of a village in any case, and Pittodrie reflected that.

Charlie Forbes the chairman had been my headmaster at Middlefield Primary, and Dick Donald, at the height of his cinema empire's success, was another of the directors at that time.

The Donald family had a long tradition in the industry and went on a spree of acquiring picture houses from other operators. It felt like they had a cinema on every corner. Dick would come into the dressing room after a game and throw tickets on the massage table for the players, with a scramble for the shows at the best cinemas. I was happy to wait and take the ones for the Astoria in Kittybrewster, just down the road from where we lived. He'd give us a lift into town after a match, travelling in style, and they always did their best to look after us.

What it lacked at that time was a belief that we should be challenging the Old Firm, or even the Edinburgh clubs.

I remember losing a cup game down at East Fife, one we were expected to win, and Dick appearing whistling a merry tune. As bizarre as it sounds, that was a final straw for me – it was like it didn't matter to the club if we won or lost. I remember speaking to him about it after and I realise I got that wrong, he was just doing what he could to try and lift the spirits and keep things upbeat. That was his way.

Douglas Philip was another of the directors who looked out for me – he always claimed to be the one who discovered me in fact. He had a printing business and, like the others on the board, had money behind him. When I was leaving Pittodrie to sign for Rangers he flagged me down on the road outside the City Hospital, just along from the ground, and tried his best to persuade me to stay – whatever I wanted, I could have it. My mind was made up though, as much as I appreciated his determination.

By the time I made that move to Glasgow in 1966 I'd been unsettled for years. With Tommy Pearson as Aberdeen manager, early in my time in the first team, I'd let my frustrations with the club's lack of ambition get the better of me and was one of a handful, including Charlie Cooke, who had requested a transfer. That was rejected, but we kept pushing and eventually they relented – although in the end I stayed for another couple of years after that.

There was attention from England – Wolves, Newcastle United, Swansea, Middlesbrough and Sheffield United were credited with an interest at that stage – but nothing that got me excited from a football perspective, and I was prepared to wait for the right opportunity.

I knew deep down what it was that I wanted and, not for the first time in my football career, there was a family influence at play. Not Hughie or Doug this time but the eldest of the Smith brothers, Jim.

Jim died in 1963 when I was making my way as a professional. He was in his 20s and it was a horrendous time for the family. No parents should have to say goodbye to their children, and for the three of us brothers left behind it was difficult to comprehend that he wouldn't be there for us anymore.

Jim was the big brother, the strong one, the one we turned to when we needed advice – but he was taken far too young. It was the weekend of President Kennedy's assassination, and I was down in Dumfries with the Aberdeen squad when I got the call to say he had taken ill at home. I got back up the road as he was being taken away by ambulance, going to hospital to get better we thought. It was a heart condition and I'm sure today he would have had a transplant and recovered. Instead, we lost him.

Jim was a Rangers supporter, and I'd gone to games at Pittodrie with him to see the likes of George Young in those immaculate blue shirts. There was something special about those games, and I always promised him I'd play for Rangers one day. Unfortunately, he didn't get to see it, but I kept my word.

Nothing worth having comes easily, and that was the case with the move to Ibrox. It turned into a Scottish football soap opera – complete with clandestine meetings, secret phone conversations and ending in a classic game of cat and mouse with the press.

Long before the Bosman ruling, the clubs essentially held players captive. As long as they offered you the same terms as you were on, they could retain you as a player. The only way out was if you were surplus to requirements or a fee was paid. In hindsight it's incredible that system stayed in place for so long.

Contracts through the 1960s and 1970s were no more than two or three pages and just about every clause was designed to protect the club, usually at the expense of the player. I've still got copies of some of them, and there are elements that you just wouldn't countenance in any walk of life now.

For example, the player would 'have no claim for wages for any period in which he may be unable through illness to implement the obligations' of the contract. There was an undertaking not to take part in any form of journalism, and the club had the right to terminate the contract at 28 days' notice on the rather vague basis of any 'reasonable ground'.

Quite rightly there were clauses that related to 'unpunctuality, disobedience, intoxication or other misconduct'. The only one in there that would have caused me any difficulty would be punctuality – although when it came to football I was always on time, it was just everything else that I tended to arrive fashionably late for. I'd call that good use of time; you don't want to waste it by being early.

It was also set down in black and white that 'the player shall do everything in his power to get and keep himself in good physical condition' and would 'use his utmost skill' while representing the club. That's a clause that could be interpreted in different ways for different players!

Those contracts were standard issue across Scottish football – the only blanks were for the club details and the personal terms. Even the bonuses were left at the discretion of the club rather than set out in the paperwork.

With everything skewed in favour of the clubs, there was no chance I would be allowed to leave Aberdeen without a fight – my star was rising and talk of a move really started to grow in the 1965/66 season.

I'd played for the Scottish League select against the English equivalent in Newcastle and stood out in that game, which turned out to be a very good shop window. That team featured four of the 11 who won the World Cup for England, although Jimmy Greaves did play that day and scored. We outclassed them though, winning 3-1 thanks to a goal from Andy Penman and a Joe McBride double.

Eddie Turnbull came to that match to give me a lift straight back up the road – he was obviously worried I wouldn't come back! I'll always remember him meeting me as I walked down the stairs at St James' Park with John Greig, and telling John not to get used to playing with me because I wouldn't be joining him at Ibrox. I thought to myself, *We'll see about that.*

Bill Nicholson, the Tottenham manager, had flown up a couple of times after that to watch me in games against Partick Thistle and then at Kilmarnock. Everton were interested too. At the same time, Willie Telfer, scouting for Rangers, had also been trailing me, and the speculation was constant for a period of time.

It went as far as Real Madrid being credited with an interest in the winter of 1965. They had been drawn to play Kilmarnock in Europe and when they came over to watch Killie in advance of those ties it was Aberdeen they were playing.

I had a good day at the office, and the Real manager Miguel Munoz, a formidable player and captain of the club in his day, singled me out as the man of the match and was full of praise – describing my performance as 'tremendous' and 'international class'. He was joined at Pittodrie by George Stirrup – a fedora-wearing, cigar-smoking English agent who had struck up a relationship with Real and acted as their man in the UK – and there was a flurry of media attention on the back of our win against Killie.

It stretched on far beyond that one game and began to gather momentum. Madrid were embarking on a rebuilding exercise and the Scottish market had piqued their interest.

When they came back to play Kilmarnock at Rugby Park, the president, Santiago Bernabeu, was very deliberate in throwing a few stones to see what ripples they caused. He spoke of a dossier of players they wanted to build their new team around and he said my name and Charlie Cooke were top of the list.

Charlie was really blossoming after moving from Pittodrie to Dundee. Rangers had been keen, but, believe it or not, Dundee had outmuscled them financially. They paid £40,000 for Charlie and made that back and more when he went on to Chelsea. Charlie had infuriated the Aberdeen support on occasions – he never liked to beat a man once if he could go back and beat him again – but there was no doubting his ability.

On top of that, he was an infectious character. Charlie had come away from home on the west coast as a Greenock boy and landed in Aberdeen to try and carve out a career for himself. He was like a breath of fresh air in so many ways, full of confidence on and off the park even as a rookie.

The thought of the two of us lining up together in the white of Real Madrid is an interesting one. I think we would have done okay!

The truth is I never really paid attention to that particular link, but the noise and rumours closer to home were very difficult to ignore.

It was unsettling, not in a playing sense but on a personal level. I've never been able to let go of something if I feel I've been wronged, and it started to feel that way at Aberdeen. The chairman was adamant they were building a team and weren't going to sell. I was just a pawn in the middle.

Eventually I asked for a transfer, just as I had done a few years earlier. That was rejected. I asked again. The same answer. A third time – the same response. A fourth – no change in the club's position.

I'd given good service, bearing in mind they had paid all of £25 to bring me in from the juniors as a youngster, and they knew they would get a big fee. Still there was no sign of any movement and I wasn't prepared to roll over.

The closest I got to honours with Aberdeen was in my last season, when we made the Scottish Cup semi-final and came out of the hat with Rangers.

It was my first experience of a big cup tie at Hampden, with all the hype and expectation that went with it. After the build-up, we ended up playing out a 0-0 draw – it felt like a chance lost for everyone in that Dons dressing room. We'd been the better side, and Rangers were booed off the pitch that day. It was a chance for me to show I could play on the big stage and against a Rangers team that included all of the big hitters. I did exactly that.

We met back at Hampden just three days later for the replay and again gave a good account of ourselves. I had a particularly good night. We fell a goal behind early on when Jim Forrest scored but equalised through Harry Melrose before half-time. You could sense the tension creeping into the Rangers team with the prospect of a second replay in store. As it happened,

George McLean knocked home a late winner to set up an Old Firm final, a case of so near yet so far for us. It may be that my performance over those two games, when the pressure was on, helped convince Scot Symon that I could add to his Rangers squad.

At the end of that 1965/66 season, I rejected the contract offer on the table at Aberdeen, but they still held all the cards. I either walked away from football altogether or signed back on. Initially I agreed to month-to-month deals, knowing it was only ever going to be a means to an end.

It came to a head in the summer of 1966 – I made it clear I wouldn't sign on again, even a monthly deal. The one option I had up my sleeve was going abroad, which was a loophole in the transfer rules, and I made it known I was willing to do that. For me, it was a point of principle – and eventually there was a reluctant acceptance that offers would be invited.

Spurs and Bill Nicholson were back watching me, and Crystal Palace too came up for a scouting mission when we played Manchester City in a pre-season friendly. We won 2-1 and I scored the winner from the penalty spot – an eventful match, with our big skipper Ally Shewan having a real battle with Mike Summerbee. Ally didn't do 'friendly'!

Tottenham had signed Terry Venables by that point, and that looked to have filled the midfield berth they had, but they maintained their interest. The Everton option was bubbling away as well, and there were some initial talks. Both were ambitious and had designs on winning the league.

I knew Forbes and his fellow Aberdeen directors wanted me to go to England. For one they didn't want to sell to a rival, for another they were certain they could get a bigger fee from clubs south of the border.

At the same time my big brother Doug was in a similar stalemate with Dundee United. He knew his worth and was quite rightly holding out for a deal that was right for him. Despite a lot of bluster from the manager Jerry Kerr, it was no surprise to me when they did push the boat out and came to an agreement that paved the way for Doug to spend the rest of his career at Tannadice.

For me, new pastures were a certainty – but it needed a few things to click into place.

That began in unremarkable surroundings but in esteemed company. Jim Rodger, a real doyen of Scottish football writing who worked for the *Daily Express*, *Daily Record* and *Daily Mirror* over a long and illustrious career, had travelled up to Aberdeen and invited me to meet him at a guesthouse near Pittodrie.

When Jim called, you didn't tend to say no. He knew everyone in the game and everything that was going on, and it wasn't uncommon for the better connected of the journalists to act as the unofficial go-betweens in transfers. That was still the case up until relatively recently, although the contact between players and the media has been reduced to more of a business-like relationship and the personal interaction has been stripped away with the advent of media conferences and the introduction of public-relations minders. We considered the reporters as friends and vice versa – bonds were built on trust.

I went to see Jim, who was holding court with Denis Law during a trip back home for a summer visit, and he told me that Rangers wanted to take me south. I told him straight away I was interested – and within minutes I was having a phone conversation with the chairman John Lawrence. That was the first contact I had and the moment it was clear in my mind where my future lay. The problem was how to make that happen.

Encouraged by our conversation, the Rangers machine whirred into action – but they found out they had a fight on their hands.

Aberdeen were holding out for something in the region of £70,000 – it was a huge price tag around my neck and not too many clubs were prepared to part with that type of money. To put it in context, the most Rangers had ever spent up to that point was £27,500 to take George McLean from St Mirren three years earlier. It wasn't about breaking records, it was potentially shattering them.

For Rangers, there was a sense of being held to ransom, and there were Scottish football politics at play. John Lawrence was a shrewd chairman, and he wasn't comfortable with the way gate money was split at that time: fifty-fifty. It meant the Old Firm were subsidising every other club, whereas in England the split was 87.5 per cent in favour of the home team. Far more palatable to the big clubs and it meant by default they could afford to pay the bigger fees and higher wages.

Sunderland had paid in the region of £70,000 for Jim Baxter, which was undoubtedly in Aberdeen's thoughts. Dundee had brought in around the same for Alan Gilzean when he moved south to Spurs. In 1965 there was a flow of Scottish players moving over the border – 17 in that one year alone – and the Pittodrie board wanted a slice of that.

On the Aberdeen side the key men were Forbes, as chairman, and the manager Eddie Turnbull.

I knew from personal experience the negotiations wouldn't be easy – knowing Mr Forbes as my headmaster, I appreciated he was a hard taskmaster!

As for Turnbull, he told me in no uncertain terms that I wasn't going to Rangers and pushed me to speak to Harry Catterick at Everton and Bill Nicholson at Tottenham. I did, out of courtesy, but I wasn't going to be bullied. The money on offer down there was eye-opening and eye-watering in equal measure – at Aberdeen I was on £28 a week, a princely £4 more than the rest of the squad by virtue of the protracted back and forth there had been in previous years when it came to contract talks.

The English sides could blow Scottish clubs out of the water, including the Old Firm, and with a business head on you would have chosen Spurs or Everton – but I was prepared to go with my heart.

Turnbull wasn't amused (he didn't like to be told no), but it was nothing personal. In fact, working with him, even for the short time we spent together, was enjoyable. He was different to the managers who had gone before, a coach first and foremost. He was the right man to take Aberdeen forward and had progressive ideas. The day I eventually signed for Rangers he was getting ready to head to Munich to go to the German sports institute, always looking to learn and bring new ideas.

I've always felt the game should be played a certain way, and Turnbull's style suited me. It was Eddie who first switched to a 4-2-4, and as one of the two in midfield I had the energy to cover a lot of ground, so I was enjoying my football more than ever.

It felt as though Aberdeen were in safe hands, but I wasn't swayed by the argument that I should have stayed longer.

To say the stubborn pursuit of the move to Rangers didn't go down well is an understatement. After I'd made the switch, I used to come home to the North-east by train after a weekend game, and Aberdeen would be in the same carriage. Turnbull wouldn't let them speak to me. He would usher them past me to their seats and try to keep us apart for the rest of the journey.

That happened for a whole season, until I bumped into him the following summer while I was walking through the city centre in Aberdeen. Turnbull beeped his horn and stopped to speak to me; from then on we were like best friends. Time can be a great healer.

It wasn't the outcome he wanted, but I know he understood my reasons for moving on and the lure of Rangers. In the end there was no bad blood between the manager and me or the chairman and the club.

I say *in the end* because at the time it felt like a never-ending saga. After months and months of back and forth, the clubs eventually met in the middle – £45,000 was the magic number.

My transfer came at the same time as Alex Smith made his move from Dunfermline for £35,000 – so Lawrence and the board were making a statement, breaking the club record twice in quick succession. It was a real signal of intent and didn't stop there, bearing in mind Colin Stein became the first £100,000 player through the door just a few years later.

When it did happen, it was all a bit of a whirlwind. Scot Symon had made enquiries over a long period of time but needed the go-ahead from the directors to push the deal through – they knew the numbers Aberdeen were seeking, and the board, to their credit, backed the manager's judgement.

Symon got the approval he was looking for while he was at Hampden for a Glasgow Merchants' Charity Cup tie between a select from the city and Leeds United. He phoned Turnbull that night to fix up a meeting in Perth the next day.

I arrived at Pittodrie for training on the Friday, none the wiser. My name was on the team sheet pinned to the wall when I arrived, but it all turned around quickly. Davie Shaw, the trainer, let me know when I turned up that there had been a change of plan, and that I needed to go and see the manager.

I went through to his office and was told everything had been settled with Rangers and we had to meet in Perth to finalise the deal. Turnbull told me to be at the Station Hotel by 1 p.m. – given it was noon already there was not a chance I'd be on time. What was that about 'unpunctuality'?

It was a case of getting there as quickly as I could. The manager and chairman were going down too, but they didn't offer me a lift – it was all still a bit raw for them.

Technically, we were heading south for talks, but I had no doubt in my mind what the outcome would be – so much so that I took my boots with me from Pittodrie there and then so I could carry on to Glasgow and get started. There was no turning back!

I know Symon appreciated that commitment, and it must have been the easiest negotiation he ever took part in. The fee had been all but agreed over the phone, the manager and chairman were there to rubber stamp it, and I didn't even ask what the terms would be. It was the move I wanted, and money wasn't the motivation. I trusted Rangers to look after me.

The press knew the wheels were in motion and, long before mobile phones, had been calling through to the hotel reception trying to speak to the manager. They were told he wasn't there – Symon had come through a back door, with the staff oblivious he had arrived, so the secret was safe for a bit longer. He insisted it was because it was the closest door to the car park, but I think he enjoyed keeping them hanging on and made the call to announce the transfer in his own time.

At last, it was official. The dream had become reality.

The summer of 1966 was a time of change for Scottish football – with the introduction of substitutes approved by the league, although it was very much considered a last resort to bring on a replacement. The covered enclosure at Ibrox was nearing completion when I joined, but it was a very different ground to the one I sit in now. With the sprawling terraces and capacity of nearly 80,000 it was the biggest in the division and, of course, the best then as it is now.

My first competitive game was a League Cup group match at home to Hibs, the curtain-raiser for the season. I'd played plenty of times at Ibrox, but it's a whole different experience when you're walking through the front door and heading for the home dressing room. The League Cup ties didn't tend to pull in huge crowds, but we had 40,000 in that day, and that type of backing is what really hits home that you're operating on a different level now.

There was a lot of attention on Alex Smith and me. We were the ones being charged with sparking a revival after a couple of difficult years. It was a strange kind of game, but a script that became familiar over the years and is still the same story today.

We had what felt like all of the ball and created a barrowload of chances but were up against a stubborn defence. We were into the last ten minutes and seemingly drawing a blank when we finally got a breakthrough, George McLean doing what he did best and hammering home a shot after Alex Smith's initial effort was turned away. Me? I played my way into the game, found my feet and got some good write-ups for my efforts – the consensus was that the two Smiths had shown enough promise to suggest brighter days were around the corner.

We already had five cup games under our belt by the time the league season kicked off, and I felt like I was hitting my stride. Partick Thistle provided the opposition – and the new recruits chipped in with a goal each, outdone completely by Mr McLean who rattled in four as we won 6-1 to go top of the league.

If I needed any reminder of the standards demanded of Rangers players it was that day – four goals wasn't enough to stop George getting a hard time from the crowd, who clearly wanted a bit more from him! It was a typical late summer day in Scotland – pouring with rain and a sodden pitch. Alex got his first league goal in his first outing, opening the scoring early on, and I chipped in with the third of our goals – linking up with Willie Johnston and firing home the cleanest of strikes after a lovely one-two. It was a nice way to open the Rangers account. As much as the goal sticks in my mind, it was the celebrations after it that meant the most.

If the fans thought they would be getting a goal a game they were mistaken. I only scored one more that season, and it was a penalty, away to Airdrie to earn a 1-0 win late in the campaign. Davie Provan was the regular penalty taker, but I was never shy in putting myself forward for those and I ended up with the ball in my hands after Wille Henderson had been fouled. The keeper got a hand to it – one of those slow-motion moments – but it had enough pace on it to whip into the net.

We weren't short of willing penalty takers. George McLean, John Greig, Kai Johansen and I all took them during that period. Later Andy Penman was on duty for a spell and Willie Johnston too.

I was keen to grab any opportunity to establish myself in that Rangers team, knowing that I had to make a big impression early. What I didn't appreciate was that I'd arrived in time for one of the most dramatic periods in the club's history.

FOUR

'THE FOUNDATIONS WERE LAID IN NUREMBERG'

AS MUCH AS 1972 is embedded in Rangers folklore, it's impossible to separate that incredible year from another that looms large in the club's history for very different reasons: 1967.

I was there. There for Berwick and the ignominy of that infamous Scottish Cup upset. There in Nuremberg when our Continental hopes were shattered in the cruellest of fashions in the final of the European Cup Winners' Cup against Bayern Munich.

When we gathered together deep in the Nou Camp for the '72 final against Dynamo Moscow there were three survivors from the cup tie and four from the European final of 1967.

John Greig, Willie Johnston and I had been through that turmoil in Berwick and were joined by Sandy Jardine in the side to face Bayern. If ever there's something to bring you together it's that type of shared experience.

It sounds a stretch to claim events five years earlier could motivate you, but believe me the chance to lay those ghosts to rest wasn't lost on the four of us. If anything, the passage of time only intensified that desire to set things straight.

Although the cup defeat at Berwick is the one that still makes the headlines more than 50 years on, it was defeat against Bayern Munich in the European Cup Winners' Cup later that year that hurt more, and that was the motivation in Barcelona. We had lived with the pain of missing out. To go through it again would have been devastating.

That isn't me trying to deflect from the impact of Berwick, far from it. The fall-out from that game ultimately cost us the European trophy.

Nor would I try and gloss over it. I doubt I'm alone in saying that I remember the bad games in far more vivid detail than I do the good ones.

That match at Shielfield Park on 28 January 1967 sticks in the mind for all the wrong reasons. Not that I'll ever be allowed to forget it even if I wanted to.

Whether it remains the biggest cup upset of all time is one you could argue either way. Celtic against Clyde in 2006 and Caley Thistle in 2000 must be up there. Hearts at Brora Rangers in 2021 is another to add to the list of contenders.

Because it was the mighty Rangers, the Berwick game will always be held up as the gold standard of cup upsets. I understand that.

It was a dark day for Rangers and for every single one of us who played that day. That said, I consider myself one of the fortunate ones – I survived it.

Jim Forrest and George McLean were the unlucky two who became the very public scapegoats, which was a massive injustice. There were 11 of us on the pitch, and it was in very simple terms one of those days when nothing we tried worked. Rather than dwell on that, you have to have the grace to credit Berwick with the game of their lives. Berwick Rangers 1 Rangers 0.

When the final whistle went the feeling was no different than in any other game that you lost while wearing a Rangers jersey

– crushing. In that sense, every defeat was equal in my eyes. We were expected to win them all.

Very soon after, you began to realise this one was different. Inside and outside the club there was a sense of disbelief surrounding it, and I've no reason to doubt the long-standing feeling that the directive to drop Jim and George, and eventually push them out of the door, came from the very top.

I think it's also fair to say it was the beginning of the end for Scot Symon – he was on borrowed time from that point on, although a European trophy would surely have saved him.

The dressing rooms at Shielfield aren't exactly cavernous, so there's no hiding place. You sit, in virtual silence, staring at the floor. I don't remember any voices being raised – it was an eerie feeling. The manager didn't have to say anything. We knew we'd fallen short and let an awful lot of people down.

You couldn't lay the blame at Symon's door. We'd prepared right – travelling down to the Marine Hotel at North Berwick to make sure we were rested and ready – and the team was strong. If we had played it a thousand times I doubt we would have lost again, but we did and had to own it.

Europe offered us the chance of salvation, and in so many ways it was the best of times and the worst of times.

On a personal level, that run to the final in Nuremberg was when I arrived as a Rangers player.

I could be a quiet character off the park. If I had something to say I said it, but I didn't push myself forward at all. I landed in a dressing room full of big personalities and needed to do my talking on the pitch.

There was also a shadow cast by a player who wasn't there – Jim Baxter. I stepped out of that shade in the spring of 1967 when we faced Real Zaragoza in the quarter-final of the European Cup Winners' Cup. I finally felt like that settling-in period was over. I'd arrived, and what a huge boost that was for me.

My name was up in lights after that game. It was a headline-grabbing display:

RANGERS VICTORY THANKS TO DAVE SMITH

DAVE SMITH SPARKLES AS LIGHT BLUES WIN

WONDER MAN DAVE SMITH SHATTERS ZARAGOZA

DAVE SMITH PROVES HIS WORTH WITH TOP DISPLAY

Just a few from the cuttings that give a hint of how that night at Ibrox went. The last one in particular summed it up perfectly – I'd arrived with a big price tag on my head and big boots to fill after Baxter's departure. In the space of one game, I won over the doubters.

The Spaniards came with a big reputation and having never lost to British opposition. Just as it is now, Spanish football carried a pedigree which we were supposed to be fearful of. The truth is we didn't fear anyone, that was the Rangers way.

I'd watched Zaragoza against Dundee previously, and their quality shone through. It was a different style of football than we had faced against Borussia Dortmund in the previous round – more flair than the Germans and a bit more of an edge, to put it politely. When Everton had played them earlier in the competition it was wild – their goalkeeper Gordon West was chased off the park as it descended into a brawl.

If the opposition had a vicious streak, so too did the west-coast weather. It was a horrendous night. Wind, driving rain, sleet and a pitch which was already waterlogged before we ran out. You could barely see a few feet in front of you, even with the new floodlights which were unveiled for the occasion. The mud was spilling over your boots with every step, and very few games will ever be played in conditions as bad as that. It felt at times like carrying on was touch and go.

I loved it!

I was wearing No. 6 but had freedom to roam – a position described at the time as a linkman, so not too different from playing off the striker today, between the lines, in the hole, the No. 10 role – you get the idea!

We talk so much about positions, systems and formations – but in 50 years the basic shape of teams hasn't changed dramatically. The same cogs still drive the machine.

Inside ten minutes I'd scored the opener – Alex Smith rolling it into my path from a Davie Provan ball forward, and from just inside the box I placed it low to the keeper's left.

Ten minutes later I beat him again with a curling free kick, but it was pushed back for a retake by the referee because he was still patrolling things in the box.

We did score again before half-time, and I was involved again, nipping in to cut it back for Alex Willoughby to tuck away the second of the night after the keeper had spilled the ball.

I had another long-range shot well saved, and it felt like everything I tried came off.

The late great Ken Gallacher described it in the *Daily Record* as the performance of 'a supreme soccer artist'. The Real captain said post-match, 'On this display he rates with the best in Europe.' Who am I to argue?

In all seriousness, it was a coming-of-age moment for me. I'd gone from a player of promise to one established on the European stage and I didn't look back.

Alex Cameron, another of the legendary newspaper men, was one of those who homed in on that 90 minutes in the rain. To win the approval of Chiefy, as he was known, was another step in the right direction. You shouldn't underestimate the power the press held.

In an article headlined 'Dave Smith kills the Baxter ghost' he wrote: 'The taunting ghost of Jim Baxter has at last been expelled from Ibrox by the man bought expressly for this purpose – Dave Smith, from Aberdeen.

'Man's inhumanity to man finally bundled all the memories, the nostalgia and the regrets down on to a lifeless Ibrox pitch, swept by wind, rain and sleet, and let the talented Mr Smith do the rest.

'He was, even manager Scot Symon conceded, a brilliant player on the night against Zaragoza, of Spain. He was compared to Baxter and then finally was accepted as having superseded him.'

Those comparisons with Baxter had started when I arrived and followed me for a long time. It wasn't something that troubled me – I didn't set out to be the next Jim Baxter, I was 100 per cent focused on being my own man. Despite what the papers may have said, we were different players and very different characters.

Of course, winning the approval of people in high places was welcome – and I probably didn't realise at the time how it would influence things in the future.

One of the admirers on the back of that game against Zaragoza was Willie Waddell, then in his role as a football writer for the *Daily Express*.

Waddell's review of the game read: 'Dave Smith has arrived as a Ranger. Sixty-five thousand saw him win his Ibrox "blue" with an outstanding performance.'

He went on to add: 'After seven months of struggling and striving, excelling and flopping, Smith has at last been accepted at Rangers class – a hackneyed phrase, maybe, but still the accolade of high-class efficiency. Smith has won this distinction because of his skill, his polish and style, and, perhaps even more so, because of his ability to set the pattern for those around him. He proved he had this by dictating the flow of the game against Zaragoza in the tense atmosphere of European competition. This is when the real quality shows, the sign of the top craftsmen when he proves his worth against accepted top class opposition.'

He continued by quoting Billy Steel while imparting advice on what I had to do: 'It is tough getting to the top, but even more difficult staying there.'

I'm not too sure about my future manager's claim that I had flopped at any stage, but football is all about opinions, and you take the rough with the smooth.

Waddell too drew comparisons with Baxter in that piece – or 'you know who' as he referred to him, seemingly not in glowing terms.

The truth was I wasn't in the least bit preoccupied by what had gone before me. It was all about what was ahead. European football was a huge attraction.

I relished playing against the Continental teams, something I was never going to be able to do regularly as an Aberdeen player. It was a chance to learn and grow as a player, a test against more technical players than we typically faced on domestic duty.

The result in Glasgow gave us the platform to go to Spain with a real belief we could finish the job, and we did that – just!

If the home leg was one to remember, the return was one that sticks in my mind for very different reasons. Before the advent of the away-goal rule, we fell to a 2-0 defeat and had to rely on the luck of a coin toss to book our place in the semi-final. I had the chance to win it by more traditional means but missed from the penalty spot with the tie level at 2-2. There were few more relieved men than me on the plane back home.

I wasn't exactly a globetrotter when I arrived at Ibrox, so European football was a big lure for me.

When we went into the draw for the opening round of the European Cup Winners' Cup there were lots of interesting potential ties to be had – Galatasaray of Turkey, Spartak Moscow of the USSR, Fiorentina of Italy, AEK Athens of Greece. Some intriguing trips on the cards.

We landed Glentoran!

As much as I've enjoyed the trips to Belfast I've made over the years, it wasn't the destination of choice from the perspective of catching some late summer sun.

What it lacked in exotic passport stamps, it made up for in atmosphere – tens of thousands greeted us at The Oval. Unfortunately, a cricket score was never on the cards.

Rangers hadn't played Glentoran for more than 60 years, and it was a massive occasion. All around the ground the streets were gridlocked. They'd never seen a crowd like it before or after. Figures differ depending on where you look – anything from 40,000 to 55,000 in a ground that was probably built to accommodate a tenth of that. Whatever the number, it's a record which still stands, and somewhere in the region of 10,000 of those there that night had made the trip over from Scotland.

We were held to a 1-1 draw – not the start I was hoping for on my European adventures. George McLean had scored for us, but Glentoran got a late equaliser, and we took it back to Glasgow to finish the tie off. That was more in keeping with what was expected, a 4-0 win including my second goal in Rangers colours on a night of torrential rain.

We went on to defeat Borussia Dortmund 2-1 over two legs to tee up the meeting with Zaragoza in the last eight, and then that coin toss set us up for the semi-final against Slavia Sofia, a tie we were clear favourites for as much because of the lack of knowledge of Bulgarian football as any technical analysis. Given PFC CSKA reached the semi-finals of the European Cup the same year, there was obviously quality in their league.

We travelled out to Sofia for the first leg, and I've got two abiding memories: a horrendous pitch in what was the national stadium, and an even worse offside decision that denied me my third goal of that European run. We were a goal up through Davie Wilson when I ran in and scored what looked to everyone like a legitimate second, but the referee took an eternity before ruling it out.

As it happened, we didn't need it. A single goal in each of the games, with Willie Henderson scoring back at Ibrox a fortnight later, put us through 2-0 on aggregate.

And so we went on to Nuremberg to face the mighty Bayern Munich on their home soil in Bavaria in the final. If anything, the venue just added to the glamour of the tie. We certainly didn't view it as a huge disadvantage to be playing in Germany in front of what was naturally going to be a partisan crowd.

You have to remember we were coming off a pretty devastating end to the league season. The final game was a 2-2 draw at home to Celtic, but it was a dead rubber by then. We missed out on the title by three points, so even if we'd beaten them we would still have been a point behind in the days of two points for a win.

The damage had been done in the previous two games when we drew at home to Clyde – who actually finished third, so it wasn't necessarily a shock result – and then away to Dundee. Given they were a top-six side, it was a tough sprint to the finish line, and we just couldn't get there with it in our own hands.

Bizarrely, it was Dunfermline Athletic who cost us the championship in the end. We lost only three games that season in the league – one at Celtic and home and away to Dunfermline. With the best will in the world, we shouldn't have been dropping points to that side, even if they were a decent team who tended to challenge at the right end of the table.

That challenge for top spot was a new experience for me – the best finish I'd had at Aberdeen was sixth, four years previously – and from a personal perspective it was a massive blow. I'd made the move to win things and to come so close and see it slip away like that isn't something you can just put to one side and forget about.

Between that Old Firm game and the European final there was a huge gap – 25 days to be precise. The way the Continental calendars failed to synchronise was a major disadvantage for us, particularly when you consider Bayern Munich played right through May and were match fit for the final.

What did we do? Jumped on a plane and headed for Canada! A trip halfway around the world maybe doesn't sound like the best idea when you've got the biggest game of the season approaching, but the travel didn't bother us. It was fine to get away and have something to keep us occupied in what would otherwise have been down time.

The focal point was an exhibition match against Sparta Prague, billed as 'world class soccer' and hosted by Toronto City. There was a big appetite in Canada for European football, and more than 21,000 turned out for a late evening game, organised by the club's ambitious owner Steve Stavro. He'd brought Stanley Matthews and Danny Blanchflower over when he was setting up the club, as well as the Scotland captain Tommy Younger. In later years he went on to own the Toronto Maple Leafs ice hockey team, funded by his business empire.

Stavro, born in Macedonia, saw the potential in bringing touring teams across and I dare say it was a deal the Rangers directors couldn't say no to.

Sparta were coming off the back of winning the Czechoslovakian league and it was a good standard of opposition given what we were working towards. Too good as it turned out – they beat us 1-0, and not for the first time in that latter part of the campaign we struggled to take our chances.

We tormented them, Willie Henderson in particular, and were raining efforts in from all angles. Nothing broke for us though.

Sparta had scored within minutes of the game kicking off and sat in to frustrate us for the rest of the match. They kicked everything that moved, and some that didn't, and it was typical of how some games against European opposition could go. The art of the professional foul was certainly not lost on them, and we had a scare when Willie Johnston was stretchered off.

Other than the result, one of the other legacies of the defeat at Berwick earlier in the season was a horrific injury to Bud. He'd gone in to challenge Jock Wallace, in the Berwick goal at that time, and come off second best – rushed to hospital with a broken ankle, to add injury to insult. Jock went in to take Bud out and never did apologise. He'd joke about it in training after joining us at Ibrox.

As ridiculous as it sounds, we took Bud back with us in the bus to get him to the Victoria Infirmary for the ankle to be set.

It would have been a quiet journey back across to Glasgow if it hadn't been for his cursing and the occasional scream of pain when we hit a bump in the road. We bundled him off the bus and into Scot Symon's car when we got to Ibrox. There was me in the passenger seat, the manager driving, and Bud, still in excruciating pain, in the back rudely interrupting our civilised conversation in the front with his full vocabulary! It's fair to say Symon was more than a little preoccupied with the result, the gravity of it starting to sink in for him.

Bud had made it back in time for the last league game and was still working his way back to full fitness out in Canada. We all feared the worst when he went down, but it proved to be just a knock. That was a huge relief given the attacking issues we already had – it was vital that we had him available, and it was a difficult balance between not rushing him back but giving him the game time to get back up to speed after almost four months out of the side.

When we returned to home soil we had a couple of other matches to keep us ticking over, winning 2-1 at Morton and then drawing 1-1 at Motherwell in Charlie Aitken's testimonial – with Dave Mackay, borrowed from Spurs for the occasion, guesting for the hosts and scoring their goal. Bobby Watson and Roger Hynd got the goals at Cappielow, and big Roger scored at Fir Park – probably making the manager's mind up about how he planned to approach the game in Germany, which was then just a week away.

They were pretty low-key performances from a team perspective, but I was happy with my own form. The hope was that everything would click into place in Germany for us.

While we were trying to stay on track with bounce games, Bayern were still in the thick of things in the Bundesliga. They signed off with a 3-0 win against Hamburg the weekend before the final, and we knew they were in decent form.

They were a club on the up and had been promoted to the top league two seasons earlier, going on to finish third at the first attempt and winning the cup that gained them a place in Europe. Their Yugoslavian coach Zlatko Cajkovski was a young pup compared to the managers we were used to in Scotland – still in his early 40s and carving out a reputation as a shrewd operator. He was the one who really built the core of the team which went on to dominate for the next decade.

Gerd Müller had been tearing it up, scoring 28 goals in 32 league matches and finishing with eight in nine European appearances, and Rainer Ohlhauser was the other big threat.

The Städtisches Stadion was an impressive venue, home to Nuremberg in the Bundesliga and one of the biggest grounds in the country. Just under 70,000 packed in for the game – one of the biggest crowds for a European Cup Winners' Cup final in the history of the competition. Only the 80,000 inside Ibrox for the first leg of the Rangers v. Fiorentina final in 1961, the 98,000 who saw West Ham conquer 1860 Munich in 1965 and the 100,000 who watched Barcelona defeat Standard Liege at the Nou Camp in 1982 beat it.

Like so many of the big grounds at that time, there was a running track around the pitch, complete with shot putt behind one of the goals, with big open stands curving around. It was a brilliant atmosphere and a real sense of occasion – the only thing missing was the result.

The experience of playing in that final was, for a 23-year old not long in the door, incredible. The pomp, the ceremony, the expectation – it all came crashing together in the best possible way.

We flew into Nuremberg but stayed out in the countryside, as became something of a tradition on our European trips. Keeping us away from the supporters and the hustle and bustle of the city centre was obviously the thinking, but when you're greeted at every airport by noisy Rangers fans it's difficult to escape the buzz surrounding the big games.

That was the case when we touched down in Germany, two days in advance of the final. We trained in the evening, although when I look back at the preparation for that game and contrast it with the way we were primed for the final in '72 it is like night and day.

I don't know if you ever played the game 'Into the water, out of the water' when you were young. It's the one where you follow the instructions and you're out if you step on the wrong side of the line, the sort of game you might play at a children's birthday party after pass the parcel and musical chairs. Believe it or not, that was part of the training routine before we took on the might of Bayern Munich!

Regardless of the pre-match routine, the promise from the manager to the supporters was that he would be playing his strongest team.

That, unfortunately, wasn't strictly true. What Symon did was play the strongest team available to him, the side he was allowed to choose.

Anyone who knows me will appreciate that I love a quiz. So, a few Nuremberg-related questions for you.

Who were the six ever-present players in the nine European Cup Winners' Cup ties that season, including the final?

Who was the top scorer in that run?

What was the starting 11 which faced Bayern Munich in the biggest match in the club's history up to that point?

My guess would be that very few, if any, could answer those three questions. Why? Because we didn't win on the night and, quite rightly, nobody remembers the nearly men at Rangers.

For completeness, the answer to Question 1 is: Kai Johansen, Davie Provan, John Greig, Willie Henderson, Alex Smith and I were those who played every game.

George McLean and I were the top scorers, with two goals each. That tells you something about the goalscoring issues which ultimately cost us the trophy.

Whereas the Barcelona team can be reeled off by every supporter of a certain age and many who weren't even born in '72, the side from 1967 is a far less familiar one: Norrie Martin, Kai Johansen, Davie Provan, Sandy Jardine, Ronnie McKinnon, John Greig, Willie Henderson, Alex Smith, Roger Hynd, Dave Smith and Willie Johnston.

All great names in the history of Rangers, but there was a missing piece of the jigsaw and Roger Hynd had been pushed into that space.

Roger was a good player in his own right and in his own position. That was centre-half, not as a centre-forward, yet it was with the No. 9 on his back that he ran out to face Bayern.

Roger gave everything he had every time he pulled on a blue jersey, and I wouldn't fault him for doing the job he was sent out to do. It was a decision the manager made, although everyone believes his hand was forced with the exile of McLean and Forrest after the Berwick result.

I say everyone believes it because the truth was taken to the grave. The only men who really know are Symon and John

Lawrence. Neither spoke about what really went on behind the scenes, at least not as far as I'm aware.

On the eve of the cup final the chairman did make remarks about the lack of forward players and seemed to be almost conceding defeat. I think that was just clumsy rather than premeditated or a dig at the manager, but at least the issues were being acknowledged. In time, they addressed that with the big spending on Colin Stein – so some good did come from what unfolded in Germany.

If Jim Forrest had been playing we would have won that game, I've got absolutely no doubt about that. If George McLean had played we would have had every chance of getting a positive result. They didn't, and the rest is history.

What I also can't fathom to this day is why Davie Wilson wasn't involved. Although he left for Dundee United in the summer, Davie was still at the club at that point and had an eye for goal. I'm convinced he could have given us a cutting edge when we were so short of attacking options. I suppose it came down to the goals Roger had scored in the league and friendlies after being tried as a forward. It was a different level of opponent to Bayern Munich.

I remember going to the byline and cutting it back for him early in the final and he fluffed his shot. Jim or George would have had it in the net in a blink of an eye.

To compare and contrast, Bayern lined up with Gerd Müller leading the line as they set about building the team that would go on to dominate European football. This was their first European final and turned out to be the first trophy of many on the big stage.

Müller played that game by virtue of getting permission to turn out with a protective shield after suffering a broken arm, something that dominated the pre-match build-up from a media perspective.

He wasn't the only big name in the 11 – with Sepp Maier, Franz Beckenbauer and Franz Roth just some of the major hitters.

We ran them so close and certainly weren't outplayed – the result tells that story. No goals after 90 minutes and the killer blow from Roth in the second half of extra time to win the match 1-0 was just about as close as it could have been.

Watching that match now is surreal. It's such a long time ago, but you're catapulted back in time, and bits and pieces come flooding back to you. Little movements and passages of play flash again in your mind, mixed with sections that feel like you're watching somebody else on the screen. My dad was there for the final in 1967 – I can pick him out in the crowd in the clips. It was the one and only time he travelled overseas, and it was a huge adventure for everyone who made the trip.

The German supporters swarmed onto the pitch at the final whistle, and you get swallowed up in it, the last place you want to be when you've lost the biggest game of your life. It wasn't all good-natured, with the home supporters grabbing and goading us, but I don't remember any headlines about those scenes.

It was a sickening feeling having to line up on the side of the pitch for the trophy presentation and watch Bayern lift the cup. We had no idea if we'd get another shot at it – of course we hoped we would, but in that moment it was impossible to see any positives. Even now, with everything that followed and knowing we made up for it, there's still a real sense of hurt.

We shouldn't underestimate how big it was for Bayern too. It was their first ever European trophy, and they went home to a heroes' reception, crowds lining the streets in Munich for them. Meanwhile we slipped quietly back into Glasgow to lick our wounds – a long summer holiday ahead before we could get back out on the park.

The final was a high point and a low point – a high to get there, a crushing blow to lose, especially the way we did. The positive is that the foundations of the success in Barcelona were laid in Nuremberg.

FIVE

'THE STORY THAT WE ALL WISH DID NOT HAVE TO BE TOLD'

ALL THAT 1967 brought was important in a football sense, but recalling those difficult moments on the park has never troubled me. They were only games of football.

What I find it far more difficult to talk about is the most significant event which changed us as a team, as a club and as individuals.

The Ibrox Disaster is the part of the story that we all wish did not have to be told.

It is important from a personal perspective to pay my respects to all those affected. First and foremost, to the families, loved ones and friends of the 66 who left home to support their team and never returned. To those who survived but who still bear the scars.

I will never be comfortable recounting the events which unfolded on 2 January 1971. I'm very conscious it is not my place to speak on behalf of those who suffered loss or injury.

As was the case in 1971, all those of us who were on the pitch that day can do is do our best to represent the enormous strength of feeling felt by the entire Rangers family.

It goes without saying it is the one match that pales into

insignificance, perhaps the only Old Firm derby that transcended any football rivalry given everything that followed.

The afternoon started with the usual colour and noise of the New Year fixture. It ebbed and flowed as those games so often do, but there were no goals until the closing minutes. The visitors scored first through Jimmy Johnstone before Colin Stein, converting a free kick from the left that I'd swung into the box, cancelled it out.

We thought our late late equaliser would send the supporters home content if not happy. Rangers 1 Celtic 1. Never has a scoreline been so unimportant.

The first the players knew of any issue was when we were told to take our belongings through to the treatment room and to get changed through there because they needed the dressing room for what we thought were injured supporters. We had no comprehension of the real horror of that afternoon, although there was no mistaking the air of panic that swept through the ground.

Even as we made our way out of the ground and headed for home, news was still scarce. We understood it was serious, but whether deliberately or not had been shielded from the worst. In the hours that followed the scale of the events became horrifically clear. By late evening the number of deaths was confirmed.

Hours turned to days, days turned to weeks. As players we felt so helpless, but wanted to do something, anything, which could give even the slightest bit of comfort during such black days.

Hospital visits became part of the routine. So too did the church services.

Attending the funerals of the 66 was a responsibility which we had to the families. It was the only small thing we could do. There were lists of those who had died and details of the services, so that we could share attendance between the players and ensure representation at as many as possible. I believe there were players at every funeral – that was certainly our intention.

Meeting those who had suffered such loss, the thing that stays in my mind is the way they spoke of people who had died at a place they held so dear. That was what gave many some strength.

The disaster has stayed with us all in different ways. The stories we heard of young lives cut short, people who had their whole future in front of them while we were free to go on with ours, cut right to the core.

Visiting the casualties on the wards, there was such an overwhelming sense of emotion for those who had survived but had seen friends and relatives perish. I cannot even begin to understand what that must have been like.

Those experiences changed my perspective on life. I would say they left me with a fear of dying or losing anyone close. I'm not embarrassed to say I don't handle grief well. After 1971 I stopped attending funerals for a long time. I could probably count on my fingers the number I've gone to since.

Even putting that down in words feels wrong. We were the fortunate ones and can never truly appreciate what so many suffered.

In later years we lived at Balbirnie in Fife for a spell, just a few miles from Markinch and the memorial that sits in the village as a reminder of the five boys who made the trip west to Ibrox on that January day but did not come home.

I joined members of the Glenrothes Loyal Rangers Supporters' Club for the annual service while we lived locally, and still travel down now each year. There is always a large attendance, including members of the Kirkcaldy and Leven supporters' clubs, for the memorial organised by Ronnie Bayne. So many decades later, there remains an overwhelming sense of disbelief that what should have been a normal day ended in such terrible circumstances.

Looking back at the immediate aftermath, it was important there was strong leadership from the club, and that was provided by Willie Waddell in particular. The chairman John Lawrence had been unwell at the time, and although he was present when the board met to plan the response, it was the manager who was the figurehead.

My respect for Waddell grew during that period, and I think that he, more than any individual, took a personal responsibility for what happened next and in the years which followed.

The club very quickly announced a £50,000 contribution to the disaster fund which had been established by Sir Donald Liddle, in his role as the Lord Provost of Glasgow, and more importantly set about mobilising players and officials to lend what support we could to the families and individuals affected.

The Requiem Mass at St Andrew's Cathedral just days after the disaster was the first gathering, bringing both sets of players and officials together in a congregation of around 1,200. A memorial service at Glasgow Cathedral was held soon after and, for that short window, a whole city and nation were united. The futility of football rivalry was laid bare, and it was incredibly moving to see.

I know it is something Colin Stein has spoken about with great feeling, but there was a deep sense of guilt for those of us who played that day on so many levels. The suggestion that our equaliser, a goal which Colin and I were both involved in, had caused a surge of supporters turning on Stairway 13 and back into the stadium was one which lingered until the public inquiry finally dispelled that theory. Your mind races with 'what ifs' – could it have been different? Regardless of the cause, the fact that people had lost their lives simply because they came to support their team left football feeling very hollow.

Understandably, there was scrutiny of the club and its actions. The decision to limit capacity for the match to 80,000 was highlighted as an indication of the proactive approach to safety at Ibrox, but I don't think anyone, with the benefit of hindsight, would argue that more could not have been done to protect supporters at every ground in that era. Rangers in particular had opportunities to learn from previous incidents in that part of the ground, and that was a source of great regret.

As far as Waddell was concerned, he made it his mission to improve Ibrox, and creation of the all-seated stadium that we know today was the result.

For the players, we had to try and get back to some sense of normality in a short space of time. The familiarity of old routines helped with that, and we had only a two-week break from playing between the disaster and the match against Dundee United at Ibrox on 16 January.

It was a very eerie feeling being back out on the pitch and similarly for the supporters who returned to the terraces for the first time. Having my brother Doug there, playing alongside Walter Smith in the United team that day, brought some comfort in what was such an emotional day. We played with a freedom that afternoon, probably one of our best performances in a long time – a combination of the release of playing and the realisation that there were far bigger and more important things in the world than 22 men kicking a ball around.

Not only for us but for everyone around the club and the city, football provided an escape. A proposal for a benefit match, to add to the disaster fund, between an Old Firm select and a Scotland side at Hampden quickly gathered pace.

I played in that unique Glasgow team that night, bolstered by some all-star names from south of the border. We lined up with Peter Bonetti of Chelsea in goal and a back four of Sandy Jardine, John Greig, Billy McNeill and me. Bobby Murdoch and Bobby Charlton were in the middle of the park, with Willie Henderson and Willie Johnston alongside George Best and John Hughes, a late replacement for Jimmy Johnstone, in attack.

Scotland won 2-1, scoring early through Archie Gemmill and then late through Peter Lorimer after Best had equalised in-between. George was on fine form that day, and it provided a little bit of light during such dark days.

More than 81,000 spectators turned out – being cheered off the pitch by both sets of Old Firm supporters was something none of had experienced before or would again.

It raised in excess of £40,000 for the fund. That was far more important than anything that transpired on the pitch, although no money in the world could have compensated for the pain and suffering the families endured.

Equally, nothing the team went on to achieve would undo that heartbreak, but the memory of the 66 we lost from the Rangers family was undoubtedly a motivation in all that followed.

SIX

'THE BATTLE TO GET BACK ON THE PITCH'

FOR EVERYONE AT Rangers the end of the 1970/71 season could not come quickly enough. Playing on after the disaster was difficult, and the reset in the summer provided a chance for the club to properly take stock and regroup.

As individuals, football had been put firmly in perspective.

I'm very reticent to claim any setback from a playing perspective was anything more than that. I had a few in that period, but in the grand scheme of things they were no more than bumps in the road.

There was also a sense of understanding the importance of the good times when they came, and the European run in '72 was something we could share with the supporters who had been through so much.

If Nuremberg in May 1967 provided the foundation, the rest of the building blocks fell into place in the months and years that followed as our style of play evolved and the moving parts began to come together to form the machine that powered its way through to the final in '72.

One of the key cogs that's often been spoken about in the run to Barcelona is the role of the sweeper in Willie Waddell's blueprint.

It wasn't that Rangers hadn't played with a spare man at the back before, it was more about the emphasis on using that position as the focal point for attacking rather than solely defending.

That responsibility fell to me, and it was one I thrived on.

It was Waddell who honed the system, particularly with the attention to detail in how we implemented it in Europe, but I'd like to think Scot Symon, at home in Glasgow as we celebrated in Spain, took some quiet satisfaction from the part he had played.

It was Symon who first dropped me back in to play as a sweeper, and I'll forever be thankful for that.

I wasn't particularly tall, and I didn't have the brute force of the typical Scottish stopper. I prided myself on not having to tackle and very rarely headed the ball. I was never once booked in more than 700 senior games (well, I was once but that was rescinded).

A lack of pace was levelled at me too, something I found a bit tiresome, and I think was more to do with my long stride and gait. I don't remember anyone running away from me, although I don't recall too many foot races in any case. If you're playing catch-up something's gone wrong. It's your brain that makes you fast on a football pitch – not just your legs.

Symon looked at all of that and saw a defender in the making!

Apart from a very brief spell as a youngster playing as a full-back, I'd spent my entire footballing life as a midfielder.

That changed in September 1967 when Celtic came calling. It was the first Old Firm game of the league season and we won 1-0 thanks to Orjan Persson's mazy run and shot in the second half – but that goal and the result were a sideshow really.

The main talking point was a horrific challenge by Bertie Auld which broke Davie Provan's leg inside the first five minutes of what proved to be a brutal match. Incredibly, the referee, Willie Syme, kept his cards in his pocket and it left the door open for a battle. The players had to help carry Davie off the pitch, and it didn't take an X-ray to know that it was a serious one, made far worse by the fact it was intentional and it was cowardly.

What the injury to Davie did do was force a reshuffle and, with Bobby Watson coming on, I dropped in to play behind Ronnie McKinnon. What started as an in-game stopgap to tide us over turned out to be career-changing for me. It was a position which suited me, where I could use the qualities I had. I don't think too many fans, or coaches for that matter, would have had me down as a defender.

It felt as though I was breaking through all over again, with a lot of attention from outside the club on the switch of position and a lot of praise with it.

I think it was the fact it came as a surprise to so many which caused the stir. As I've touched upon I was as far from a typical Scottish defender as you could get, but to the credit of Symon and the managers who followed they looked beyond the norm and tried something different.

It was new for me, but I never felt like I needed a period of adjustment. Having the whole of the game in front of you is different from being in the midfield, where you're playing on the half turn, and I thrived on it.

What I would concede is that by the time we got to Barcelona in '72 I had hit my peak with impeccable timing.

For three or four seasons I shuffled between midfield and defence, but that season I was the sweeper that Waddell needed to make his system work.

I was older and wiser in the role and had the confidence to throw off the shackles. Initially when I dropped back I probably put too much focus on the defensive side of the job, but over time I began to put more emphasis on what I could add going forward, and it added a new dimension to my play.

I also benefited from playing behind some fantastic centre halves. Ronnie McKinnon, Colin Jackson and Derek Johnstone had their own unique qualities, but I had a brilliant understanding with all three. I knew I could trust them to do the defensive work, and it gave me the freedom to play.

The understanding with Peter McCloy was crucial too; the pass-back rule wasn't in play so having that option as an out ball was ideal.

There was a game against Hibs at Easter Road early in the 1971/72 season which was an acid test for the manager's approach, and we passed it with flying colours. It was a real blood-and-thunder game and Hibs had us pinned back for large swathes of it, before we hit them with a sucker punch in the dying seconds through Colin Stein.

Waddell came in after the match and told me it was the best he had ever seen me play. Given he wasn't one to give compliments loosely, I was happy to take it.

Inter Milan's Armando Pichhi, Franz Beckenbauer, Bobby Moore – the comparisons were all coming out in the press. It was flattering at the time and even more so when you look back.

I admired Moore especially for his style – despite the criticism he sometimes got. He's rightly remembered as a legend now, but it's easy to forget that the England captain wasn't always valued when he was at his peak or even after his retirement. Sadly, I think it was after his death that the real appreciation for all that he achieved and brought to the game really came to the fore.

Defenders stepping out with the ball cause all sorts of problems. Do you commit to close them down or do you let them break? The frustration I have now is seeing those situations developing in games and central defenders carrying it 30 or 40 yards before turning back or passing sideways. There's too much fear and not enough willingness to back their own ability.

Carrying the ball was part of it, but an effective sweeper has to play like a quarterback and make the in-game calls about the 'plays'. Having the ability to mix it up is crucial, and my passing range was probably my greatest strength. There's a lot of talk in football about long balls and short passing and which is better. To me there are only two types of passes: good or bad! If you can land a pass from 70 yards onto a forward's instep it's a great tool to have, and that was something that I was able to build my game around when I dropped further back.

Shelling a ball 70 yards to nobody, in the direction you're facing, is a completely different story, and unfortunately we laud too many defenders who have a tendency to do that.

Nobody taught me how to play the position, it wasn't coached – we just went out there and did our thing. It wasn't a case that the way Symon expected me to approach it was different to Waddell or Wallace after him, it was on us as individuals to adapt and grow into the roles we were expected to play.

If you put me into the side in place of Colin Jackson, for example, the way the team played would be slightly different because every individual sees the game differently – or they did. Today, with the more rigid structures and tactical approaches, a player has to adapt their game to fit the plan, and the danger is you lose that individuality.

I've seen it said that I was before my time, that I would have been better suited to a different era. I'm not so sure that's the case. I don't think I could have played without the freedom that we were so lucky to have.

Watching teams now you can see the patterns of play and that they have been drilled within an inch of their lives. Goal kick routines – from goalkeeper to centre-half, to full-back to centre-half, back to the full-back and up the line – are so predictable. The playbook of corner kicks is the same, and even in open play you can quickly decipher the passing tempo, the off-the-ball running and rotation.

That's all held up as a sign of a well-coached team, which it's difficult to argue with – it's almost beyond coaching and into the realms of choreography. My granddaughter Mia is a ballerina and it's incredible to see from a young age the precision that you can get a dance troupe to move with. They practise every step and every movement until it is second nature – the beauty is the synchronisation and the margin for error is tiny.

The game is in danger of going too far in that direction. If you set some of the goal kicks to music you would find they barely skip a beat in terms of when and where the ball is moved.

There has to be room for spontaneity and for decision-making on the park. More and more it's about following the patterns, and you'll see players looking to the touchline for instruction. They've become reliant on being told what to do and when to do it, like painting by numbers.

The huge part of my game, and of so many in our side, was the ability to play off the cuff. For me, the sweeper role was a joy because I had licence to roam but also because I was credited with the ability to read the game.

You see that quality written about so often, as if it's a sixth sense. It's a bit more complicated than that, but to try and boil it down I would say it is about being willing to take a risk – in and out of possession. So often for me it was a case of thinking what other defenders would do in a particular situation and doing pretty much the opposite. The opposition play to what they expect. If you do something different – drop a few yards deeper or press higher, dribble rather than pass – and call it right you make the interception or you spring an attack. If you play safe and do what's predictable, you lose that opportunity.

It was no different for the likes of Willie Johnston on the wing. Doing the unexpected was what put the fear of death into full-backs. If they knew he was going to follow a pattern of play or play narrow, where the game is congested in the middle of the park, they would have been absolutely delighted. Defenders love safety in numbers. What they hate is being isolated one-on-

one in a wide area where a winger can get past them and to the byline.

That freedom to break forward was a big part of how I played the role of sweeper. Barcelona demonstrated that, but it wasn't unique to that game.

I didn't score too many goals (14 for Rangers in fact), but I remember one in particular against Dundee United at Ibrox in February 1972 when I was playing as our last man. It was 0-0 going into the last five minutes, and I made a run from sweeper as Tommy McLean picked up the ball. Tommy slipped it in front of me and I knocked it past the United defence and ran on to glide it through their keeper Hamish McAlpine's legs. Jim McLean had taken over as manager at Tannadice and they were going well, so it was an important win for us.

It was described as the type of spell a player dreams of, and I wouldn't argue with that assessment.

In domestic football and in Europe it felt like everything I touched turned to gold, something that felt out of reach a few months earlier.

When the season began I was clawing my way back to fitness after my second leg break in the space of 11 months.

The 1971/72 season and everything it brought, for the team and personally, had extra significance for me because of the battle I'd had just to get back on the pitch.

Those two leg breaks inside a year had knocked me for six, just as I was coming into my prime. I was 26 when I suffered the first one and the time I spent out was a huge frustration both in terms of the chase for honours with Rangers but also my hopes of forcing my way into the Scotland set-up.

The first injury was in a game against Kilmarnock at Rugby Park in April 1970. We were a goal up and on course to take that into the break when I was caught in a challenge with Ross Mathie over on the enclosure side.

I knew it was a serious one, a difficult sensation to put into words but very different from a knock or a muscle injury. I was pretty robust physically – I don't ever remember missing a game through injury other than those two leg breaks and went on to play competitively well into my 40s. But I suppose if you're going to do it you may as well do it in style. The worst thing was it was my left leg – the important one!

It was a freak accident. There was never any blame apportioned to Ross, and I had him in my squad at Berwick Rangers in later years. After hanging up his boots Ross went on to spend a long time as part of the SFA age-group coaching set-up.

We were challenging at a throw-in and his heel caught my leg and it was just a dull pain. I went to stand up, thinking it was just a knock, and fell back to the ground. I couldn't put any weight on it and that darkness when you're about to black out came over me, a dizzy sickening feeling that masks the pain.

I was carried off to the side of the park, tended to by the physio Tommy Craig and assistant trainer Joe Craven with the game raging on. There was a penalty awarded to each side, so not a quiet afternoon.

They made a call for medical assistance over the tannoy and ended up with four doctors queuing up to help, so I was in good hands.

We went on to draw 2-2, but by then I was at Kilmarnock Infirmary for X-rays.

As I was taken away on a stretcher and into the ambulance I don't think I fully understood what had happened, but the medics were already treating it as a break.

It confirmed what I already feared, a fractured tibia was the diagnosis. The only piece of fortune was that it was a clean break, so the doctors were relatively upbeat about what they saw.

I was kept in overnight and able to make a call home – although too late to catch my wife Sheila, who was waiting as usual at the top of the road in Newton Mearns to meet me from the team bus. This time it didn't stop and just sailed past! She was walking back down the road, pushing our baby daughter Amanda in her pram, when a neighbour stopped to say, 'It's a shame about Dave.' That was the first she knew.

Because it was a straightforward fracture, they were able to put me in plaster and discharge me the next day. Willie Waddell visited on his way home, and the club doctor was positive I would be back in time for the new season, which is what I wanted to hear.

My brother Doug had a bad ankle fracture in his early days and went on to play more than 600 games for Dundee United, so I knew at first hand that it didn't need to be career-ending.

It was a full cast, over the knee, so the leg was straight – the pain soon subsided, but the inconvenience didn't. Just getting around the house was an effort, so it was a relief when that eventually came off and I got a smaller cast in its place. I was able to bend my knee again and it started to feel like the comeback was getting nearer.

By that stage I could hobble about without a stick, so it was progress, and it meant I could get back to Ibrox more freely and keep in touch with the manager and the boys. That first visit back was important. You don't realise how much you miss that environment until you're kept away from it.

The coaching staff knew I was a good trainer, and I never carried any weight when I came back for pre-season, so they had plans to get me back up to speed quickly. Tommy Craig, in typically methodical fashion, had a recovery schedule plotted out for me, and I followed it to the letter.

The final cast came off after three weeks, and then it was a case of learning how to walk again – even over the course of three or four months the muscles waste away and it's a very strange feeling having to take those baby steps.

The check when the cast came off didn't seem overly scientific. The doctor grabbed my leg, put it under his armpit and gave it a good shake. When it passed that test I was good to go!

From there the training picked up, primarily in the gym with more weights and rope work to keep the focus on upper body while the leg was still settling. Rehab can be a lonely existence, so without wishing ill on anyone it can be nice to have a bit of company. I was working my way back at the same time as Graham Fyfe and, towards the final stages, Alfie Conn and Sandy Jardine, so we were able to push each other along.

From the gym it was on to jogging around the pitch, running and eventually back into full sessions and contact. I was helped by the fact Jock Wallace's regime meant the full-time players were kept in training after the season had ended, so I was back in time to catch the last of those sessions before a short break for the squad.

We cancelled our holiday plans and I stayed at home to work on my own. By the time we flew out to Sweden for the pre-season tour that year, I was fit and ready to go. After long periods of working alone, it was brilliant to be back in the group and it felt like the worst was behind me.

Fast-forward to March 1971 and it was back to square one. This time it was my right leg, and it was a challenge in training that did the damage, playing a bounce game on the old ash pitch at the Albion.

It's incredible to think the club had hundreds of thousands of pounds' worth of playing assets working out daily on blaes, but we didn't think anything of it. There was a grass pitch there too, but we did most of our work between the running track at Ibrox and the red ash at the Albion.

For a treat we'd be taken to a junior pitch to work on, or down to Largs and latterly Troon. As well as the track around the pitch for running and fitness work, there was a small indoor area under the stand that we used for sprint work as well as a small gym deep in the stadium. Maybe it's not a surprise we didn't spend all of our days working out, and why today's players are such finely tuned athletes in comparison!

We were considered fortunate to have our own training ground next to the stadium, but when you look back there were missed opportunities to improve the facilities and create the equivalent of Auchenhowie much earlier that it eventually came to fruition.

As far back as the late 1960s Sunderland had the foresight to create a bespoke training complex, but it took decades for clubs on both sides of the border to catch up. Sunderland are on their third purpose-built centre now, improving every time.

I don't think the Albion pitch was the cause of my leg break, but it maybe did play a part. What I can say with certainty is that it was mainly my own fault.

It was 0-0 in the training game we were playing, and Jock Wallace was away to blow the whistle to send us back in, but I persuaded him to play next goal the winner. As we played on, Willie Henderson and I went in for a challenge and our legs got tangled. I fell forward and there was a crunch. Looking down I could see my foot facing the wrong way – unlike the first time when it had been a clean break, this was very much in the stomach-churning category.

I was becoming familiar with the inside of ambulances and was whisked away to the Victoria Infirmary to be put back together.

Our own orthopaedic consultant, Mr Archie McDougall, was on duty down at East Kilbride so by chance it was Celtic's doctor who was assigned to me. I was there on the bed in my Rangers training kit, and he was talking through what needed to happen, recommending immediate surgery to insert a steel pin to bring the bone together and encourage it to heal.

Tommy Craig, who had travelled with me, was nervous about it. I was in a lot of pain, but he was adamant we should wait for our doctor to arrive. I'm glad we did. He examined me a little while later and said if it had been pinned I would never have played again.

Instead, he put me under with anaesthetic and reset the leg before plastering it up. On the plus side it was a smaller plaster this time, so easier to get around, and I consider myself fortunate that on both occasions my legs healed without a hitch.

I was made to wear strapping down round my ankle after the second one, although I'm not sure what difference that would have made if the bone had popped out again. I've never really had any problems since other than a bit of discomfort now and again. Whether that's down to the break or just wear and tear I don't know, there are plenty of others suffering far worse than me with arthritis and the legacy of cortisone injections.

It was worse than before in that there were multiple fractures, but better in the sense I'd been over the course already. I knew what lay ahead, and although it wasn't appealing, there was less of the unknown.

If it had been the same leg I'd have been more concerned because there's always that nagging worry that the bone won't heal properly and will go again. Having had a good few months back playing, those concerns were well behind me by the time I was back with the other leg in plaster.

It was the same slog, trying to keep myself ticking over with upper body exercises until I could get back on the training field and in the gym properly.

Tommy Craig had come in as physio as part of Willie Waddell's backroom reshuffle and he built up the medical department to something that was unrivalled at that time – the best equipment and the knowledge to go with it.

Tommy had been a medical student before turning to physiotherapy and had put in a long football apprenticeship in the juniors. He was still only in his 20s when he came to us but had a mature approach to the job. He quickly built up an understanding of each of us as individuals and where our strengths and weaknesses were physically, with his notes covering everything from injury history to our resting heart rate.

Stringent pre-season medicals, including X-rays and cardiograms, were introduced – two before every campaign started – and we had regular check-ups through the course of the year. We had ultra-violet lamps, which we were told would guard against colds, and got regular flu jabs before that was the norm. Halibut liver oil tablets kept our joints in good order.

Then there was the special potion we had rubbed into our heads pre-match, a mix of water and whatever the magic ingredients were. I'm convinced that's why I lost my hair so early!

Between that and being hosed down with cold water before and after training sessions, it was certainly an experience.

If Jock Wallace was the bad cop from a training perspective, Tommy was the good guy who was there to put us back together after a trip to what was dubbed Murder Hill. More on that later.

When we travelled overseas, Tommy was laden with medical bags and all sorts of kit. He didn't like to leave anything to chance, although how he cleared customs I'll never know.

We were very fortunate to have the best treatment and the best conditions to perform – right down to the protein shakes served up by sprint coach Tom Patterson. Egg, milk and a dash of sherry was the magic recipe and it was designed to help build muscle. It became part and parcel of the speed training we would do in blocks through the season, with afternoons set aside after the normal work had been done.

It wasn't the only time there's been sherry in a dressing room I've been involved in. Jimmy Hogg at Aberdeen used to swear by a slug of it pre-match, and before big games as manager at Berwick I was known to serve small glasses to the players, to settle the nerves and put a bit of fire in the belly on a cold day.

I've never been a drinker, but for me it was about using anything that took their mind off any tension they might have and it caused a bit of chatter among the players which helped loosen things up. A few of them still mention it now, so I'm going to say it did the job I wanted it to!

Given the situation I found myself in with the second leg break, I couldn't have been in a better place or in safer hands with a forward-thinking coaching staff at Ibrox. It wasn't unusual to have coaches from other countries dropping in to observe training the Rangers way, so the reputation for attention to detail was obviously growing outside of Scotland.

The recovery from injury went to plan, but getting back into the side was a bigger challenge than I'd imagined. Early in the 1971/72 season I was back on the park and playing in reserve games, and I expected to push back into the first team quickly. It didn't work out that way for me. I had to fight for that place.

It was a new experience for me, and I like to think I did things the right way. I would spend a couple of hours extra at Ibrox in the afternoon, building fitness but also confidence in the strength of the leg. I had a routine of running with the ball at speed and firing off shots or passes, repeating it over and over again. I felt ready, and my body wasn't sending any warning signs.

I didn't treat playing for the reserves any differently than I did in the big games, and it was a pleasure to be able to work with some of the young players who were coming through at that time. For the likes of Derek Parlane, it wouldn't be long before the call came to make the step up.

As a side note, even after that I didn't wear shinguards. There was a bit of clamour around that time from the coaches and trainers for everyone at the club to use them, but like so many others I found them cumbersome. Do I think guards would have made any difference with my leg breaks? Not at all – they might have protected against cuts and studs being raked down the shin, but the way they were put together meant they didn't have a big bearing when it came to high impact.

There were definitely more similar injuries in that era. The lack of shin guards was maybe part of the problem, but I think the ferocity of the tackling, coupled with the sturdiness of the boots, would have been a bigger factor. Neither of those were at play in the case of my injuries though.

I lost 18 months of my career to those breaks, but I count myself lucky that I was able to come back from them unscathed, aside from the bump in my shin that's still there as a little reminder.

When I did get back in, it was a case of making up for lost time — and the games came thick and fast as that incredible season took shape.

SEVEN

'FROM THE GLOOM CAME SOME LIGHT'

THE ROAD TO Barcelona was long, it was winding and it was a wonderful ride to be on. It lasted eight months, took us to the heart of the European game's most powerful nations, and was packed with incident and accident as we navigated that path to the Nou Camp.

The first-round match away to Rennes was the start of the journey, and there was a focus in everything we did. Nobody knew the path we were on, but there was a determination from the very outset.

The attention to detail was there from day one. It set the tone for everything that followed, and it was the work that was done on the training field, unseen by the supporters or the media who followed us near and far, that was instrumental to what we achieved.

I can be dismissive of the impact of coaching and managers, even when it comes to my own career in that side of the game.

That's because I didn't like to be coached. As I've already touched upon, I performed at my best when I had freedom, and we had a few I'd argue were exactly the same. Willie Johnston is the obvious one – could you teach what Bud had? Could you make him better by giving him instructions? Not a chance. He was a free spirit who played spontaneously.

What I wouldn't dispute is that every individual is different. As much as Bud and I railed against convention, there were plenty of others who thrived on structure, and what we had that season was the perfect blend between both, especially in Europe.

Domestically, you could say the tactical approach was light touch. We were expected to win against every team in the league, and I include Celtic in that. The focus was always on what we were going to do and how we imposed ourselves on the opposition.

When it came to the European Cup Winners' Cup tie, there was a definite change in emphasis from Willie Waddell which cascaded down through the coaching staff.

He was fastidious when it came to watching the opposition, and the research he did in advance of every tie, no matter how difficult that was in an era when travel was less easy and video footage was hard to come by.

He took that scouting information and turned it into a battle plan. The away legs were always the key – if we could take something from those games we backed ourselves to do the business at Ibrox.

Before every game we would be drilled on the opposition. From shape and attitude through to individual players and how we would deal with them.

Raymond Keruzore, a midfielder on his way to becoming a French international and a Rennes legend, was among those singled out. André Betta, who had scored the winner in the Coupe de France final against Lyon to earn their place in the competition, had already been capped by then and was another on the list for close attention. Philippe Terrier, was another.

Alex MacDonald and Willie Mathieson were two of the go-to men in our side when it came to man-marking, and that was the case against Rennes, where both were given that responsibility.

Willie, so often unsung, was crucial to so much of that run to the final. He had what I'd class as his best season – physically faster and stronger than ever and adding more of an attacking threat to balance the defensive qualities which everyone recognised.

We spent entire sessions in preparation for Rennes, working on that one-on-one approach in areas of the park for pressing them all over the pitch.

It wasn't all hard graft. Being back on the road again always brought the buzz, and the balance between work and fun was good.

For Rennes we stayed out in the countryside at the Hôtel Ar Milin on the edge of the village of Châteaubourg, surrounded by woodland but with plenty to keep us busy – a boating lake and go-kart track for starters. We had glorious weather out there and in-between training sessions were able to get out to the shops and generally to relax away from the goldfish bowl of Glasgow.

When we turned up for the match we were met with a group of fans who were asking after tickets for the game. It turned out they'd run out of cash, so we had a whip-round on the bus to help them pay their way in. We must be the only team in Rangers history who had to pay fans to watch us, although you could argue there were a few over the years who maybe should have done!

The game itself went pretty much to plan. We came away with the 1-1 draw thanks to Bud's goal and had something solid to build on for the return on home soil. I was watching from the sidelines, on my way back from the leg break, and it was a match we could have won. We had chances, despite getting some criticism for being cagey.

The return at Ibrox was a case of managing the tie and making sure we built on the foundations laid in France. It was brought forward a day because of Celtic's tie against Copenhagen 1903 and the policing arrangements for both games, but the shorter rest period didn't do any harm at all.

The 1-0 win, courtesy of Alex MacDonald's well-taken goal as he followed up on another shot from Bud, was a case of job done. It wasn't spectacular, but it was never in doubt over the course of the two legs.

For me, that Tuesday night game was another to watch from the stands, but I was edging closer. I'd been eased back into the first team when we played Aberdeen on the Saturday before the Rennes tie, but Ronnie McKinnon came back into the side for the midweek tie.

We lost that game against Aberdeen, but coming through the 90 minutes was a win on a personal level. It marked the beginning of the best season of my life and laid the foundations to push my way into the team for the rest of the European run.

Rennes was a game we were expected to win, although among the players there was that expectation we would win every match which goes with the territory at Ibrox.

French football was in a transitional period at that stage, and although individually there were good players in their ranks, as a unit there was always the feeling we would be too strong for them.

Sporting Lisbon, for those on the outside looking in, was a different prospect, and when our name came out with them in the second-round draw it was one that caught the imagination straight away.

Sporting were a powerhouse domestically and carried a reputation worldwide, with all the reports we got of a very solid counter-attacking team with quality from 1 to 11.

From the goalkeeper Vitor Damas, a Portuguese international, through to Argentinian striker Hector Yazalde and the young forward Chico Faria, who went on to play for his country, there were danger men who were pinpointed as we prepared for the first leg.

Yazalde was the star man, on and off the park. He was small, tricky and a real handful. Looking back at his record for Sporting,

104 goals in 104 games gives a hint of what he was all about, and it was no surprise that he played, and scored, for Argentina in the 1974 World Cup finals as well as winning a European Golden Boot along the way.

The one that was most intriguing was another Portuguese international in Joaquim Dinis. Over 6ft tall and unorthodox in his style, he was the polar opposite to the typical Scottish winger and something very different for Sandy Jardine to contend with.

In typical Sandy style, it didn't faze him in the slightest – he had made his debut for Scotland against Portugal at Hampden just the week before the first leg, and Tommy Docherty had tasked him with man-marking Eusébio, which he did very well in a 2-1 win for the home side. It wasn't Sandy's natural game (I'd say he was far better suited to having freedom to get forward), but he was one of those who could play anywhere and do it well.

Their coach, Fernando Vaz, came over to watch us against East Fife. He was a bit taken aback by the crowd, who understandably were pushing for better after an indifferent start to the league season. The concept of a team being booed in a match they won was obviously new to him, but again it's a reflection of the high standards every Rangers player should be held to.

I'd never be critical of the support for demanding more. It's what makes Rangers different from other clubs, and playing under that type of pressure certainly drove me on.

The preparation, as ever, was in detail. Willie Waddell travelled to watch Sporting on home soil, and the entire squad was taken to Hampden for that visit of Portugal in the build-up, although the national side played a different way to their club counterparts.

Whereas the international team played a short passing game, the word we were getting about Sporting was to expect a more direct and fast-paced approach. They had a very good blend of experience in defence and youthful energy in attack, and we were well warned it would be a close tie. I don't think anyone realised quite how close it would be.

The first leg was one of those topsy-turvy European nights at Ibrox, a raucous atmosphere and a scoreline to match. It was my first appearance in the run, and it was a brilliant first-half performance from the team to storm into a three-goal lead – only to suffer the pain of conceding two in the last 20 minutes to leave the tie in the balance going into the second game.

Colin Stein scored twice with his head and Willie Henderson fired home the third – they were well and truly rattled. Damas in the Sporting goal looked like he could be got at, and we were testing him at every opportunity. Crosses, shots and balls over the top were raining in.

But Lisbon roared back in the closing stages. There was a horrible-looking injury to Andy Penman early on, with blood pouring from a leg wound, but thankfully it turned out to be not as serious as it first appeared. Andy had a bad run of luck with injuries and deserved better fortune.

The medics were earning their wages that week. It was in training before the Sporting home game that John Greig suffered the cut to his chin that left him needing stitches – and led to the famous beard being grown for the remainder of the European campaign. We weren't allowed beards or moustaches, or hair over our collars, but John gained medical dispensation!

Pre-match preparation had been down at Largs, with the trips away a sign of how seriously the club were treating the European competitions. They wanted us rested and prepared for those ties, and the investment paid off.

Sporting were based just along the coast at Troon, so the sea air was obviously viewed as the perfect pre-match tonic.

Our base for those pre-match getaways was the Marine and Curlinghall Hotel, right on the seafront. It had grown over the years, with the two hotels joined together in the 1950s, and was run by the Logan family as one of the country's premier holiday destinations – complete with cocktail bars, a dance hall, billiards room, croquet lawn and sun loungers.

In reality its heyday was probably coming to an end when we were there – my abiding memory is of the head waiter with a coat caked in grease, although he did have the grace to put on a pristine pair of white gloves if there was a wedding or special occasion! The Marine and Curlinghall was demolished in the mid-1980s, so we won't be heading back for any reunions or silver-service dinners.

We would train at the Largs Thistle ground or on the lawn overlooking the sea, a good opportunity to be away from any distractions in Glasgow and removed from the excitement which understandably built up in the city when the big games were rolling around.

Travelling out for the return tie, I was expecting to be playing from the start. The team was going through a real purple patch domestically, goals flying in from all directions, and I'd settled back in for the matches in-between the two Sporting matches – a 4-0 win against Motherwell and 3-1 win against Kilmarnock.

Instead, it was Colin Jackson who got the nod to partner Ronnie McKinnon.

You rarely got an explanation. The team was picked and that was that. Maybe the manager was managing my game time, or possibly he wanted a more defensive option in there for what he was expecting to be a battle.

We just had to hold on to the 3-2 lead we had, a nil-nil would have done just fine. If it was uneventful the manager was aiming for, that plan fell to pieces before we even reached Portugal.

The issues we had travelling out have been well documented. What should have been a couple of short hops, from Glasgow to London then on to Lisbon, turned out to be a marathon.

When we arrived at Glasgow Airport on the Monday morning

we were told fog south of the border was going to delay our departure. No problem, you can easily kill an hour or two. So we trooped onto the plane and got settled. Then were ordered off again, with the weather still not playing ball.

It was lunchtime when we set off, and then when we neared London word started to filter back to the passengers that we weren't able to land because of a strike at Heathrow, so we ended up circling for what felt like forever.

It transpired it was the ground crew who were taking industrial action, so we had no choice but to unload the plane ourselves.

Now, bear in mind we didn't travel light for these games. It wasn't the type of workout we'd planned for.

Then we got the news that nothing was leaving Heathrow that day because of the strike, so there was a scramble among the management and directors to get an alternative. That turned out to be a charter from Stansted, so it was a bus across the city to get there, only to find out the plane hadn't made it back from Munich to pick us up.

We conceded defeat at about midnight, heading to a nearby hotel for the night before trying again the next morning. We hung around for hours waiting for the plane to arrive, and it was hardly worth it. There were serious doubts about whether it would get off the runway, it was that clapped-out.

By the time we disembarked in Portugal it was well into the evening, so we were more than a day and a half behind schedule. Not the ideal preparation for the biggest game of the season.

We were camped at the Hotel Palacio in Estoril, and it would have been nice to have a bit longer there – it was a beautiful setting just off the beach and even in November a sun trap. For the trivia fans among you, it's the hotel that is said to have inspired the Bond book *Casino Royale*, with Ian Fleming seemingly captivated by his stay there. When we travelled, we did it in style.

The Royal York in Toronto is one that sticks in the mind, a residence favoured by the Queen and other members of the royal family when on tour in Canada.

It was there that John Greig and I were subjected to a full interrogation from Willie Waddell. He hadn't long taken over as manager and obviously hadn't had the pleasure of settling the room bills – he had caught sight of the tab for the room John and I were sharing and just about fallen off his seat by all accounts. It was sitting at £1,500 after a couple of days, the price of a decent car back then.

To be fair, we'd made the mistake of dining in the finest restaurant in the hotel on the first night, with steaks falling off the plate, and after being warned off that had opted for room service – not stopping to query what the charge was for the waiter who arrived with a trolley and hot plate to cook your meal on the spot. Add to the equation we had eight or nine of the boys with us each night for food and drinks and it quickly added up. The trick on a Sunday, when you could only get a drink with a meal, was to order a round of sandwiches and a crate of beer. Then repeat.

The manager was adamant it would be coming out of our wages, but he didn't follow through with it. If you find yourself in Toronto, the Royal York comes highly recommended. Just avoid room service.

I'm not convinced the room bill at the Palacio would have been much smaller, but we deserved a treat after the trip we'd had.

If the journey to Lisbon had been a nightmare, the Estadio José Alvalade itself was a dream to play at – a huge big bowl of a ground, with a big crowd to match. With a running and cycling track around the pitch, it was very different from a cold Tuesday night in Arbroath – where you could hear every cough and spit from the stands – but there were drums and tannoys to create an atmosphere.

We'd had the chance for a short, sharp training session on the pitch earlier in the day, but that never prepares you for running out in front of 70,000.

If it was relatively civilised in the stands, there was no shortage of drama surrounding the game.

The 3-2 lead we'd taken overseas was pegged back to 3-3 midway through the first half with a Yazalde goal. You can't say we weren't warned about his sharpness in front of goal.

Then Colin Stein did what he did so often and pulled us back level on the night and ahead on aggregate. Back it swayed again, Laranjeira putting Sporting 2-1 up on the night and level at 4-4 for the tie.

Step forward Mr Stein – 2-2 with a poacher's goal, and crucially back in front on aggregate.

Then tragedy struck. Ronnie McKinnon went into a challenge with the striker Joao Lourenco and was down in a crumpled heap. I was a substitute that night and seeing Ronnie down like that was heart-breaking. I'd been through it myself twice in quick succession with leg breaks and I had a sense it was serious as soon as he hit the floor.

There was a flurry of action with the trainers and medics, and I had to get myself set to replace him. Once you're on the pitch and in game mode, everything else fades into the background.

It had been played at incredible pace from kick-off, so coming into it cold was a challenge. Subs were very rarely used, unless there was a major injury, so you weren't on the bench with any real expectation of featuring.

It turned out I had longer than expected. A late goal for the home side, from Pedro Gomes, pushed it into extra time with the tie level at 5-5 as Sporting led 3-2 on the night.

A brilliant run from Willie Henderson, with his cross turned in by a defender, looked to have clinched it for us, but there was a late penalty in Sporting's favour and Fernando Peres tucked it away.

Are you keeping up? Sporting ahead 4-3, the tie level at 6-6. Full time – and then chaos.

The away goal rule had first been introduced in 1965/66, but it wasn't across the board. Some European competitions used it, including the Fairs Cup, but others didn't or only applied it in later rounds. It was a mess.

We knew at the back of our minds it was in place, or thought it was, but the referee had no hesitation in ordering a penalty shoot-out instead. Faced with that, you don't really think to question it – you presume the officials know the rules.

I was a regular penalty taker during my time with Rangers, so I was confident enough when I got the nod from the manager.

I went up, paused my run, the keeper dived early, I smiled as the goal opened up – and rolled it past the post. The referee didn't like the stutter in the run-up, so he pulled it back to be taken again. I did much the same again with the run-up, just speeding it up enough to get past the ref's scrutiny. Again, the keeper went early – and again I put it wide. There can't be too many who have missed twice in a penalty shoot-out, certainly not too many who have finished on the winning team.

I loved the adrenalin rush of taking penalties and always backed myself. It's a bit of a chess match. You give the keeper the eyes, pick your spot and do what you've done a thousand times before in training and in games. Only sometimes it doesn't go that way. A fraction off with the aim, a slight misplacement of your standing foot, a bobble off the turf – there's plenty of moving parts to contend with.

When they hit the net it's an incredible feeling. When they don't, your heart feels like it will sink out of the bottom of your boots.

I was in good company in Lisbon as far as the penalties were concerned. Sandy Jardine, Colin Stein and Tommy McLean all had theirs saved. There can't ever have been too many clean sheets in a shoot-out, but Damas managed it that night.

We trudged off the park that night thinking it was all over for another season. Then from the gloom came some light. The journalist John Fairgrieve came looking for Willie Waddell with a copy of the rule book, and it was there in black and white. There should never have been penalties. We were the rightful winners on away goals.

Even with that jumping out from the page, it was a nervous time. The manager sought out the UEFA representative and got confirmation that we should progress, but it still needed the rubber stamp from on high to be sure. We didn't get that word through until we touched back down in Glasgow the following day.

Ronnie was with us on the flight back, still in huge discomfort after what had been diagnosed as a double fracture. He had been operated on overnight and put a brave face on it, but the last thing you want in that condition is being hauled up plane steps on a stretcher with a long journey ahead of you. He was transferred to hospital when we got back home, not knowing what was ahead for him.

While my recovery from both leg breaks had been relatively straightforward, for Ronnie it was a long and painful process. It was never spoken about and certainly not voiced publicly, but I think we all began to fear for his future as we saw him trying to get back to playing and being hit with setbacks along the way.

When Ronnie suffered his injury it left me as the old head in the back four, and that responsibility spurred me on. I enjoyed being the organiser and the voice back there, and as that season went on I took that responsibility and ran with it.

After the physically and mentally draining events in Portugal, a holiday was in order, albeit a working one. The club had agreed we'd do a guest appearance in Israel, playing against Hapoel during a four-day stint in Tel Aviv.

The opportunity to travel and see the world wasn't lost on me, I don't think I ever took it for granted. We were able to go to

Bethlehem and see the Wailing Wall, although it wasn't all about the culture. We had an incredible hotel and sun on our backs – the perfect contrast to the cold Scottish winter.

Then came the hiatus, in European terms at least. Between playing in Lisbon at the beginning of November we had a four-month break before the quarter-final against Torino. The league carried on at full throttle, but we knew we had that tie to look forward to.

Think of Italian football and you instantly picture defensive organisation, rugged efficiency and tactical discipline.

That's the case now as it was 50 years ago, so when our name came out of the hat with Torino, we knew what to expect. Or so we thought.

Before a ball had been kicked that perception had been laid to rest, with the message coming through from the coaching team that we shouldn't expect a battle of attrition. Torino, we were told, would come at us and had the armoury to match their ambition.

Gianni Bui, a clever centre-forward and their top scorer that season, and the pacy winger Giovanni Toschi were among those picked out as the danger men. It was a team, as you would expect, packed full of quality.

They had beaten AC Milan in the Coppa Italia final to qualify for the competition, so we were well aware of their standing.

From Claudio Sala, an Italian under-23 international, and Giorgio Ferrini, the veteran Italian midfielder who had been in the national side as far back as the 1962 World Cup and is still Torino's record appearance holder, to Luciano Castellini, a keeper with a growing reputation, and Paulo Pulici, a powerful and skilful striker being tipped for big things in the game, there were star names all over the park and a core of players who had turned out for Italy whether at under-23 or full international level.

Pulici went on to be picked for the Italy squad for the next two World Cups and was top scorer domestically the season after we played them – so it turned out the reports we were getting back about his potential were on the money.

In Scotland we were well aware of Torino's reputation, particularly because of Denis Law and Joe Baker's stint with them. Players of that calibre demonstrated the ambition of the club and that was backed up by finance.

The suggestion was they would be on a bonus of £1,000 for a win. Bearing in mind you could pick yourself up a shiny nearly new Vauxhall Victor or Ford Cortina for about the same in 1972, that was a massive incentive. Although we did get win bonuses, it wasn't anywhere near that level.

Torino had sent their official Jacinto Ellena to watch us with a two-man camera crew to film the proceedings for their tactical work in the build-up to the game. Ellena singled out myself, John Greig and Derek Johnstone post-match and spoke about his concern about the power, pace and energy in our team.

Torino were chasing the eventual Serie A champions Juventus and went on to miss out by a point in the league, only losing five games. That underlines the strength and the quality they had, but their manager was very complimentary of the way we went about our business.

The choice of ground was one of the first moves in the mind games prior to the tie. Turin's own stadium was compact and more intimidating. The alternative – the Comunale Municipal ground, also used by Juventus – was a bigger and better venue but lacked the same atmosphere. Torino opted for the latter – so from that perspective it was a bonus for us before the referee's first whistle. There was still a fiery feel from the terraces, but the big open pitch suited the way we liked to play and the park, even though it hosted the Juventus v. Wolves match the night before, was suited to our passing game.

We were taken along to the Wolves game on the eve of the match, to get a feel for what we would be running out to but also to kill the boredom and any nerves which might have crept in.

We flew out as usual on the Monday morning, heading by chartered plane to Turin before making the hour's drive by coach to our hotel at Asti. Aside from the shambles which ensued on the trip to Lisbon, it was a pretty well-established routine.

Light ball-work sessions, with our hotel next to a nice training complex, and plenty of time for rest and relaxation, leisure time and the occasional trip into the local shops for souvenir hunting. Those trips built the bond we had in the group, and as the campaign went on that spirit grew stronger and stronger. The closer we got to the final, the belief also built. I'd say it was in Turin that our confidence shifted up a level.

To go to Italy and come back with a positive result would have given us a real chance of making the last four. A draw would have been classed as a good outcome, so to return with that in the bag courtesy of an away goal was a real shot in the arm. Willie Johnston's goal early in the game, after brilliant work by Willie Mathieson down the left wing, put us in the driving seat, and we held that lead until they equalised with a scrappy effort. Torino threw everything at us as they went for the win, particularly in the second half, but I always felt we limited them to half-chances and posed enough of a threat going forward.

From my own point of view, it was another one of those nights when it just clicked, in a season when it felt like everything was effortless. By that point the supporters' club player of the year awards were beginning to be handed out, and I was proud to collect a number of those – as well as getting plaudits in the press and being the subject of renewed calls for a Scotland return. That never came, but there was a bigger prize as far as I was concerned.

The European ties had a big-game feel the further we progressed. The Italians greeted us with fireworks and plenty of noise, but that was nothing compared to a packed Ibrox with the songs in full flow.

There were 75,000 flooding through the turnstiles on the night we welcomed Torino, and with the league campaign fizzling out, there was huge expectation about redemption in Europe.

Again, we had retreated to Largs to prepare. Again, we were well drilled.

Alex MacDonald grabbed what proved to be the only goal of the game after a lung-bursting dart to get into the box, this time the damage being done down the right wing with Tommy McLean's run and cross. Tommy was coming into his own as the season went on and he thrived on the games where he could beat a man and drive into space.

There were heroes all over the pitch for us, though. We shut out one of Italy's most feared attacks, a side gunning for the league title, and were controlled in everything we did.

France had been conquered, Portugal overcome and Italy swept aside. Next stop: Germany.

EIGHT

'WE DIDN'T JUST BEAT BAYERN, WE PULLED THEM APART'

IF A PICTURE is worth a thousand words then there's one image that tells the story of the pride with which I look back on my Rangers career.

It's not from the Nou Camp and the celebrations in Barcelona. It's not on the runway in Spain when we carried the trophy back on its first journey to Scotland, or the lap of honour back in Glasgow.

Instead, it was taken a month earlier. It's a picture of a legend – and of Franz Beckenbauer!

That pre-match captain's photo before we faced Bayern Munich in the second leg of the semi-final at Ibrox is the one that encapsulates everything that was great about that crazy wonderful year.

In front of a packed stadium, with 80,000 roaring us on, I shook hands with The Kaiser knowing that we were about to play the biggest 90 minutes of our lives.

Level at 1-1 after the first leg in Germany, it was make or break for our season. For some of us, make or break for our careers.

To have the honour and privilege of leading the team out for that match is the stuff schoolboy dreams are made of. That night dreams came true in so many ways. We didn't just beat Bayern, we pulled them apart.

Time had passed since we last faced them in the 1967 final, but for the group of us who had played in that match there was definitely a sense of wanting to right the wrongs.

It hurt to lose that game in Nuremberg, but that pain grew as the years went on and the realisation that those chances don't come along every day really began to sink in. Remember, I'd been at the club for less than a year when we went to Nuremberg for the game in 1967. As far as I was concerned, that's how it was at Rangers and that's how it would always be.

Five years on, there was a wonderful opportunity to replace those bad memories with great ones.

Bayern weren't just a notch up from the teams we had played. I'd go as far as to say they were the best club side in the world in our era. One of the best club sides of all time in fact.

Sepp Maier in goal, Beckenbauer in defence, Paul Breitner in midfield and Gerd Müller in attack – can anyone name me a better spine of a team? Outside of our own, of course.

They were all in their prime and an incredible unit, flying high at the top of the German league and part of a national team which would go on to win the next World Cup. Physically strong, technically excellent and intelligent footballers.

The draw suited us. Away in the first leg and the return back in Glasgow. By that stage we were settled into a rhythm and a style of play for the European games that was working.

We of course had our very own in-house translator in the shape of our reserve keeper Gerhardt Neef, back on home soil and able to keep us right. Gerry had a bit more of a Glaswegian twang than when he'd left for Scotland!

The worry in the build-up to the game in Munich was an injury John Greig had picked up the previous weekend, with his leg swollen and bruised from a crunching challenge. It was never mentioned outside of our own camp, but he probably shouldn't have played. As was so often the way, it was a case of being patched up and sent out.

There must have been half a dozen in that run to the final alone who had pain-killing injections for different injuries. Cortisone was a physio's friend, and we didn't question it. To be fair, the treatment at Rangers was far more advanced than at every other Scottish club and that's reflected in the longevity which so many of us had. Sandy Jardine played on until the age of 39 with Hearts and was Scotland's player of the year at 37, I was still playing football in my 40s and felt fit enough at 50 to give players 30 years my junior a run for their money.

Against Bayern, we went out with the intention of imposing ourselves on them rather than bowing down to them. The safe option would have been to sit in and hope to ride it out, but we were at a stage in our growth as a team where we didn't have that mindset. We were there to go toe to toe.

The old Grunwalder Stadion was another great arena, a proper football ground and full of passionate but knowledgeable fans. I say that because they actually applauded when I pulled off a couple of my trademark dribbles out of defence – so they obviously knew a player when they saw one! There are some noises you choose not to hear, but, believe me, when it's positive you soak it up.

Even when they took the lead in the first half through Breitner, we didn't buckle. The game plan was in place, and we stuck to it, with Colin Stein's shot towards goal deflected in by Rainer Zobel. At 1-1 it was another away result that gave us the chance to finish the tie at Ibrox – a brilliant platform to build from.

Back home there was no escaping the buzz. For all the might of Bayern, there was already excitement about the prospect of going to Barcelona. Supporters' clubs were even then booking up buses, travel agents were taking provisional bookings for flights, and every shop and petrol station you went into would bring another story about the plans being made for Spain.

There was, of course, the usual rush for tickets for the semi-final. The club soaked up some of the best practice from the countries we visited on that run, including on the commercial side. Advertising on tickets was introduced for the Bayern Munich semi-final, a money-spinning innovation borrowed from Torino and some of the other continental sides.

There were a few quirks which stick in my mind from that run. Seeing the flags of the opposition team's home country flying above our ground is one – it was a Rangers tradition at the time and the type of thing that set the club apart. I'd imagine some were easier to source than others!

The visitors were treated very well by the club, with gifts exchanged and the best of hospitality for directors. It was a chance for our own board to show all that was good about our institution, and with the social club opening during the course of the season there were some very progressive developments in and around Ibrox. To call it a social club is a bit of a misnomer – it was a venue in its day that was unrivalled in European football.

The *Rangers News* had been launched too, and the timing couldn't have been better. There were plenty of good news stories to focus on as Barcelona loomed. It sold well, but advertising revenue was just as important. From brewers to banks and motor traders to travel agents, there was no shortage of takers for ad space.

Not surprisingly, the Bayern tie provided plenty of good copy. It was the stuff of fairy tales really, with a few plot twists in the background.

We did the customary trip to Largs in the days leading up to the game. There was a doubt again about John Greig, after another heavy knock in our Scottish Cup semi-final against Hibs a few days earlier. We drew that game, and a replay was the last thing we needed as the end-of-season niggles began to pile up. The fact we went on to lose the rematch 2-0, on the back of the second leg against Bayern a few days earlier, was probably no surprise in hindsight.

Before Munich came calling they had John dipping in and out of the sea trying to get it fixed. Right up to the wire there was a chance he would make it, so it wasn't until the day of the game I knew I'd be leading the team out in his absence.

It was the type of tie that I lived for. Standing in the centre circle, armband around my left arm, it wasn't nerves I felt – just a massive surge of pride that made your heart swell.

I'd first been appointed vice-captain in the 1967/68 season when I led the team out for the first time against Morton that winter, with John missing through injury on the day. We won 1-0 to keep our unbeaten start to the season going. In fact, we kept that run going right the way through to the final game of the season – 90 minutes from going invincible, only to lose 2-0 to Aberdeen and, after Celtic won their final game, missing out on the title by two points. It was as close as I got to a league winner's medal, but it wasn't to be.

Being given the honour of the vice-captaincy of Rangers sounds like one of those momentous occasions, a state-of-the-nation address and rousing speeches all round. Nothing could be further from the truth! The first I knew was when the manager asked me to lead out the team just before the kick-off. By that stage you're in that game mindset and you don't really have time to think too much about it.

It's only really years later, when you look back and see the pictures with the armband on, that you realise the significance, and I'm very proud to have taken on that role. We had a team full of leaders, a fantastic group to be part of. I always joked it took me a year before I got a pass from any of them, so to be accepted as one of the senior players was a proper rite of passage.

John and I were roommates as well as captain and vice-captain. Initially I'd been paired up with Bobby Watson, Alex Smith and Davie Wilson, but for my last five years at the club it was with John, and we built up a good understanding on and off the pitch.

Being entrusted with the captain's armband was another sign I was growing into the job of being a Rangers player, and it's another of those personal achievements that can't be taken away from me. It means a lot. To play for Rangers is one thing, to captain the side, even once, is a huge honour.

Whether I had the armband or not, I tried to be a leader in every game I played. That means different things to different people, but to me it was about setting an example first and foremost. Doing things the right way.

It's also about managing the game on the pitch, something that didn't always go down well back at home. Sheila didn't appreciate the pointing and the shouting when I was on the pitch. She said my arms went like a windmill. That was just in my nature, though. I was always a talker on the park and saw it like a chess game with pieces to be moved.

Derek Johnstone has told the story before of the way I cajoled him through games as a young boy playing beside me at the back, as well as his surprise at the way I would do the same with the opposition. There was a little bit of psychology at play when it came to those strikers we were up against. It caught them off guard and knocked them off their stride.

DJ speaks fondly of that time, and I hope he did benefit from the experience. The truth is he didn't need it. He was a fine football player and a good reader of the game, with the pace and power to match. It was a pleasure to play alongside him.

I was proud to be given the responsibility of captaining the side in John's absence over the years that followed, and the Bayern return leg in '72, and it obviously holds very special memories for me.

Of course, it would have meant very little if we hadn't performed – but we did, and the rest is history.

There I was, a quiet boy from Aberdeen standing in the centre circle of a packed Ibrox, the blue shirt on my back and the captain's armband on my sleeve, ready to go head to head with one of the best sides world football has ever seen and shaking hands with a man worthy of his legendary status.

Everything you have seen, heard and read about Beckenbauer is justified. He was the consummate defender: cool, calm and collected. Seldom ruffled, rarely having to break stride and so comfortable with the ball at his feet.

He was the leader of a quite remarkable group that had been assembled in Munich, and the opportunity to test ourselves against them, with the stakes so high, was one to relish.

To provide a bit of context, six of the Bayern team were part of the Germany side that beat England 3-1 at Wembley just a few weeks later. Gerd Müller and Uli Hoeness both scored that day, underlining the assessment that they were world-class players in a world-class club unit.

I'd argue we won the cup at Ibrox that night. Very few outside of Ibrox gave us a chance. When we came through it, there was a feeling we were unstoppable.

When you take a step back and look at what that Bayern team accomplished, before and after '72, it's quite incredible.

Sepp Maier: Four Bundesliga titles, four domestic cups, three European Cup wins, the European Cup Winners' Cup, the World Club Cup, the World Cup, the European Championship German footballer of the year three times, more than 470 appearances for Bayern and 95 international caps. The greatest goalkeeper of all time? Certainly a very strong contender.

Franz Beckenbauer: Side by side with Maier for all of those glittering honours mentioned above, Beckenbauer was German footballer of the year four times in that golden period for the club. With almost 400 appearances for Bayern and 103 for his country, he was a captain who led by example. A World Cup-winning manager into the bargain – his reputation transcends the generations.

Herwart Koppenhofer: A league and cup winner with Bayern and a German under-23 international, he was one who flew under the radar but had his part to play in what was a formidable back line.

Georg Schwarzenbeck: A rock of a defender for club and country, he played more than 400 games for Bayern and was another who had been part of the side that beat us in the 1967 final. He went on to add three European Cup winners medals to the collection, six Bundesliga titles, three domestic cups, 44 caps, a World Cup, a European Championship, and is another who rightly has a place in Bayern's all-time 11.

Johnny Hansen: The great Dane slotted effortlessly into that all-star cast of home-grown players in Munich. Denmark's player of the year in 1967, he went on to win three league championships with Bayern, a matching set of European Cup medals as well as a domestic cup before returning home to play for Vejle Boldklub.

Franz Roth: The Bull, as he was aptly nicknamed, was the match winner against us in 1967. Something of an unsung hero, he was picked only four times by Germany but played more than 300 games for Bayern over a 12-year stint with the club. Four league titles, four domestic cups and three European Cup wins completed his collection.

Rainer Zobel: Another who was there through all the good times, Zobel racked up 180 games for the club – including all three European Cup triumphs in the 1970s. Three Bundesliga wins and a cup winner's medal completed the collection.

Paul Breitner: He was just a pup when we played against him, but Breitner was already destined for greatness. Another who can lay claim to being one of the finest players the world has ever seen, he moved on to Real Madrid only a couple of years after that match in Glasgow – but not before winning a cup, three league titles and the European Cup. Breitner returned for a second spell at Bayern and added another two Bundesliga titles and a cup to the two La Liga wins and Copa Del Rey success he had in Spain. A European Championship 1972 and the World Cup two years later, scoring in the final against Netherlands, were the major honours in 48 games for Germany.

Edgar Schneider: It was Schneider who had scored the winning goal in the German cup final to earn Bayern their place in the European Cup Winners' Cup. He only played around 60 games but collected two Bundesliga winner's medals along the way.

Uli Hoeness: Three league titles, a domestic cup, three European Cup wins, 35 caps, the European Championship and the World Cup – Hoeness has a familiar set of honours. A former president of Bayern, he's a one-club man who, like Breitner, was just a young man starting out when he crossed swords with Rangers.

Gerd Müller: The greatest goalscorer the game has ever seen? Müller came alive in the box and was the man we had most to fear from. He scored 398 goals in 453 games for Bayern – breaking just about every record along the way with club and country. Another veteran of the final in 1967, he went on to win four league titles and a matching set of cups. He starred in all three of the European Cup triumphs of that era and was at the heart of the German team for the European Championship and World Cup wins in 1972 and 1974. He was Europe's leading scorer in 1972, just as he had been two years earlier on his way to winning the Ballon d'Or. Müller, in short, was the real deal.

On a spring day in Glasgow, we reduced that all-star cast to shadows of themselves. When we saw Beckenbauer and Müller arguing with each other on the pitch at Ibrox, we knew we'd broken them.

The team that did it was: McCloy, Jardine, Mathieson, Parlane, Jackson, Smith, McLean, Johnstone, Stein, McDonald, Johnston.

The details don't need repeating, but for completeness I'll do so all the same. From the moment Sandy Jardine strode forward in the opening minute and curled home that stunning goal to put us 1-0 ahead on the night and 2-1 up on aggregate we never looked back.

The confidence was coursing through us.

Willie Johnston was unplayable – they didn't know how to handle him. Left-foot corners, right-foot corners – he was toying with them from start to finish. It was from another of Bud's deliveries into the box that Derek Parlane swept home the second, still in the first half, and we were in total control. A special mention to Derek, a teenager who played without fear and put in an incredible shift.

The atmosphere in the ground was like nothing I've ever experienced. When the goals went in it felt like the ground was shaking, from the first minute to the last the noise was deafening. That went up about 100 decibels when Bud sat on the ball, taunting some of the greats of the game. He didn't care much for reputations!

Sometimes when you play, the crowd is just background noise. This was different. Every word of the chants of 'Barcelona here we come' were crystal clear as they rang out around the ground.

It was a privilege to have been part of that occasion, to have soaked it up and breathed it in. It was a defining moment for me as a player and for the club.

NINE

'IF YOU CAN SURVIVE GULLANE, THERE'S NOTHING IN FOOTBALL TO FEAR'

AFTER THE ELATION of the win against Bayern, then came the wait. The long, long wait. Those 35 days between the victory at Ibrox and kick-off in Barcelona.

It was a time to get excited about what lay ahead, but if we could have hit fast forward we would have. The overriding feeling was one of frustration at having the pause when all we wanted to do was get on and finish what we had started.

We played out the domestic season and those bounce games against Inverness and St Mirren, but mainly it was a time for trying to nurse us through to kick-off at the Nou Camp.

We'd played 65 games prior to the final, including friendlies and the European ties, and even though the bumps and bruises were piling up there were no concerns about fitness in the group. Famously so.

The sand dunes dubbed Murder Hill at Gullane have become a symbol for Jock Wallace's training regime. Was it enjoyable? Of course not. Did it work? Yes, although not in the way that you might think.

There's a reason you don't find professional teams running up dunes today, even if some amateur sides still embrace the traditional methods. Sports science has, quite rightly, taken over, and there's a more measured approach to conditioning.

The beastings that we went through at Gullane did play a part in building stamina, although I'd argue they probably caused their share of problems too for those more prone to muscle injuries. It wasn't actually the body they had the most impact on – it was the mind.

Because of the gruelling workload and the way we were pushed to the limits, we believed we were fitter and stronger than any team at home or abroad. The psychological advantages were huge as individuals, and it also brought us together as a group. If you can survive Gullane, 90 minutes on any pitch in the world against any team doesn't hold any fears.

Aside from that, the trips to Gullane were few and far between. Most of our work was done on the training pitch, in the gym under the stand or on the track at Ibrox doing sprint work and hurdles.

It would have been at the start of the 1971/72 season that we first made the trip east, and it was everything it has been billed as and more. We got pushed to the limits and when we hit them it was a case of going again. There was no mercy, with timed individual runs and team races. Think of the bleep test but with the added fun of shifting sands under your feet and mountains to climb.

My memories of Gullane are of the sun beating down and the burning on your skin being matched by the searing pain in your calf muscles and hamstrings after the first couple of runs. I grew up with the coast on my doorstep in Aberdeen, but a dip in the North Sea was never high on the 'must do' list until it came to Gullane and trying to get some life back into the muscles.

I've never been back but maybe I'll take a more gentle stroll up the dunes for old time's sake soon, to still be able to get up them 50 years on and two hip replacements later would be an achievement. The surgeons who installed those joints in recent years said the originals had been worn away to nothing and it was put down to the years of wear and tear from training and playing, but the flip side was that I've always stayed fit, and I was back on my feet within hours of coming out of the operating theatre.

The work we did as young men has, for the most part, stood us in good stead from a health perspective, even it didn't feel like it when you were up to your knees in sand.

Just like the summer trips to Gullane became a fixture, so too did the pre-season camps in Sweden. The facilities in Scandinavia were fantastic, staying at purpose-built sites favoured by the likes of Everton and Wolves. It was a wonderful setting to tune up for the season ahead, surrounded by countryside but with everything on site which we could ask for. From sports halls to saunas to table tennis and a boating lake. There was even a ski jump, although we were ushered away from that!

Thankfully, there was more of the ball on the overseas trips than at Gullane, but still plenty of physical work, with circuit training stations dotted through the woodland trails that we did our cross-country runs on.

The work that was done in the summer of 1971 was a huge part in ensuring we were ready for what followed in May 1972. It gave us the core fitness to see us through the harsh winter and hectic travel schedule and the mental strength to go the distance.

It meant that in the time at home waiting for 24 May to roll around we weren't doing much more than keeping the legs moving and working on the technical side.

The attention to detail I've mentioned was a big part of the build-up to the final, from the pen pictures of the opposition through to the work on set-pieces that Willie Waddell loved. Me? Not so much!

I remember practising attacking corners before the Rennes tie, and he had everyone set up where he wanted them. I ended up arguing black was white with the manager – he wanted me in one place, I was adamant he was wrong. He gave up in the end. He knew I'd do what I wanted anyway, so it was a losing battle. My dad would always tell me not to argue with referees or managers because they were in charge. Generally, I heeded that advice, not always though.

Waddell and I had our moments, but actually he was a calming influence in a dressing room which had its share of fiery characters. It wasn't unusual to look over to the dugout and see him sat back smoking a cigarette, as bizarre as that sounds now. Whether we had just conceded or scored, his demeanour rarely changed.

That approach helped to keep things on an even keel when excitement was building. The reality was, whatever we did back in Glasgow, we were just killing time. When we were packed and ready to go, climbing the stairs to the plane, was when it all started to feel real.

We didn't travel light, that's for sure. If we were playing in Leith or Lisbon, there was always a giant kit hamper with two full kits and spare shorts and socks as well as all the other bits and pieces of kit, from sock ties to soap. We always changed jerseys at half-time.

For overseas trips there was all the training gear to come with us, from tracksuits to kit and towels. We wore red shirts, black shorts and white socks for training, and the coaching staff had different tracksuits to the players. Waddell in dark blue, Jock Wallace in red and Tommy Craig in light blue.

We'd take pennants and boxes of club ties for the European games, and of course a hamper full of boots and trainers – normal studs and moulded soles for each of us, with spare studs and laces packed too.

Joe Craven was the man on the coaching staff tasked with a lot of the logistics for those trips, and we had it running like clockwork by the time we departed for Spain.

We weren't kitted out specially for the occasion – we'd had suits and blazers before, but not for the final. The main dispensation was being allowed to swap jerseys at the end – that was definitely reserved for the big occasions.

Generally, we had one set of kit for the season, so had to look after it. At Ibrox you would put your training kit on a wire frame, like a full-body coat hanger, at the end of a session and pop your boots in the basket at the bottom. All of that was slid into a big drier, ready for you the next day.

There was one change for Barcelona. If you look at the team photo, we're all resplendent in our Adidas tracksuits and boots, kitted out for the occasion a few years before sponsorship deals had really become established. The strips themselves were Umbro, although the two firms had a link-up at that point so were part of the same stable.

I wore Puma boots for a long time but switched to Adidas at Rangers. I think we got £100 each for the group wearing Adidas in Barcelona, so a decent bonus to add to the mix.

By then marketing was kicking into gear and there was beginning to be some competition to their dominance. Puma had Eusébio onside, Adidas had Beckenbauer, and it was really around that time that the big brands began to exploit the size of the audience globally.

That hadn't quite filtered through to the Scottish game yet. The way it worked for us was that you went into town to the sports shop the club had a tab with and picked out your boots from whatever they had in stock, and they charged it back. We didn't have limits as such, but I think we would soon have heard about it if we were seen to be going over the top.

Mind you, once you'd worn in a pair of boots you didn't necessarily want to swap them, not least if they'd brought a bit of luck – even if they had holes in them! All you needed was a bit of strapping to patch them up and you were good to go.

The boot-room at Ibrox, a wonderful wood-panelled corner of the ground which smelled of polish and cut grass, was filled with rows and rows of pretty much the same boots – a few different Adidas styles at that time to suit different fits, but all along the same lines. You needed a bench to reach the top rows, with all of the players from first team through to the youngsters keeping their kit there; all of it, as is the Rangers way, looked after with loving care and attention.

Even in the ten years or so I'd been playing professionally, the kit had come on leaps and bounds. The boots were lighter, the leather softer and the soles more flexible. You could have them in any colour too, as long it was black with white stripes.

That did begin to change, and I took a bit of stick when I came back to Scotland from playing in America in 1976 to take over as player-manager at Berwick Rangers. I was sporting a pair of white Adidas boots with tangerine orange stripes. They were like something straight out of the Super Bowl. The boys in the Berwick dressing room must have thought I was Mr Big Time when I pulled those out of my bag, but it wasn't the fashion statement everyone thought. They were genuinely the only boots I had after travelling back from the States.

They were standard issue over there where I'd been playing with the LA Aztecs, matching the orange and white of our kit, but it was a long time before they took off on the muddy fields of Scotland. I'm not sure if I can claim to be the first to wear white north of the border – I know there were a few in England around the same time – but given the stick I got I don't think there could have been many.

I am going to pin my name on a couple of other kit innovations from my time with Berwick.

The first was squad numbers – I'd worn No. 13 with the Aztecs and chose to stick with it when I came back home. A lot of teams didn't use 13, lots still don't, and I liked to be different.

It definitely wasn't unlucky for me, given we went on to win the league and I won a couple of individual awards wearing it. It caused a lot of confusion in the first season, journalists getting the team lines always assumed I was a substitute, and there were a few hastily rewritten reports when they figured out that little Berwick were breaking convention.

At Berwick we were one of the first to attract a shirt sponsor too, on the back of appointing a recognised kit supplier for the first time. We went with Bukta for the kit deal, reintroducing the familiar black stripes after having gone with all gold tops prior to my arrival, and Spellman Audi were our proud first sponsors on the front of the kit in 1978 – six years ahead of Rangers with the CR Smith link-up.

Hibs, with Bukta as their main sponsor as well as kit supplier, pipped us to the honour of being first, but we were in a very small minority in Britain to be selling kit space in the late 1970s.

I'm pretty sure Berwick also became the first Scottish side to wear pink, around the same time. To be fair, that wasn't a deliberate choice – it was a laundry malfunction in the Smith household when our white change kit with red trim ran in the wash! The players didn't complain, not too much at least.

There was no No. 13 for Barcelona – it was the No. 6 that I'd made my own, with the kits embroidered with the European Cup Winners' Cup final markings around the badge. The bags were packed, and we were on our way.

We had a couple of training sessions planned to loosen up in advance, although whether we would get a chance to get a run out on the Nou Camp pitch was still up for debate because of fears about the surface holding up to extra footfall in the run-up to the game itself.

It's always useful to get a feel for the surface and the pitch. Whether it was Douglas Park in Hamilton or one of Europe's top stadiums, I liked to get a feel for the surroundings – a bit like

The journey begins: Proudly showing off my Aberdeen Lads' Club kit in the garden of our family home at Provost Rust Drive in the city.

Best foot forward: Honing the left foot that served me so well in training with Aberdeen. My time with the Dons proved to be the start of a football adventure. *SNS Group*

The dream move: Joining Rangers provided the opportunity to play in massive games and I thrived on the Old Firm atmosphere as well as on the European stage. *Shutterstock*

Big match: The proudest day of my life as Sheila and I were married at the St Nicholas Kirk in Aberdeen in 1967.

In action: Playing in front of the Ibrox crowd was a unique experience and one you never forget. If I could do it all again I would in a heartbeat. *Eric McCowat Sports Photography*

Setting rivalries aside: Celtic skipper Billy McNeill and I during a promotional tour we worked on together for sponsors. I valued Billy's friendship and there was a great mutual respect that bridged the Old Firm rivalry.

Home from home: Pulling on the blue jersey in the Ibrox home dressing room – a privilege that I never took for granted.

Band of brothers: European trips were a chance to bond as a group, with a brilliant camaraderie in the squad. Pictured, from left, during the trip to Italy to face Torino are: Bobby Watson, John Greig, Peter McCloy, me and Willie Mathieson.

Head to head with the Kaiser: Captaining Rangers was always a huge honour, none more so than in the semi-final victory against Bayern Munich at Ibrox in 1972. The picture of Franz Beckenbauer and me ahead of kick-off brings back great memories. *SNS Group*

Final countdown: Relaxing by the pool at the hotel at our base outside Barcelona with John Greig and Willie Mathieson. *Eric McCowat Sports Photography*

Good voice: I'm not known for my singing voice – but I was in full
flow in this picture, taken just minutes after the trophy was collected.

Party time: Once we got hold of the cup there was no way we were letting go! It came
everywhere with us, even into the giant bath at the Nou Camp. *Eric McCowat Sports Photography*

That winning feeling: Showing off the big prize with Jock Wallace, Colin Stein and Willie Mathieson. *SNS Group*

Special cargo: Sheila and I together with John Greig and his wife on the plane journey back from Barcelona, guarding the trophy more carefully than we had the night before when it suffered some damage! *Eric McCowat Sports Photography*

The winning team: Displaying the European Cup Winners' Cup we worked
so hard to bring back to Glasgow. *Eric McCowat Sports Photography*

Crowning glory: Receiving the Scottish Football Writers Association Player of the Year award in 1972,
presented here by former Prime Minister Harold Wilson on the night, capped an incredible season.

Rare collection: My gold and silver medals from the 1972 and 1967 European Cup Winners' Cup final are cherished mementos of my eight years at Ibrox.

The American dream: In action for the LA Aztecs, resplendent in white boots and wearing my lucky No.13, against Alan Willey of the Minnesota Kicks.

Champions at last: A Berwick Rangers team picture following the title winning 1978/79 season, with playing kit swapped for manager's suit for the occasion. We were one of the first clubs in Scotland to embrace shirt sponsorship. *SNS Group*

Black and gold: In action as player-manager for Berwick Rangers against Rangers in a pre-season friendly in 1979 as we prepared for life in the First Division. I turned 36 that term but had no intention of hanging up the boots. *SNS Group*

Together again: The Rangers tie against Barcelona in 2007 gave the 1972 squad the perfect opportunity to reunite in Spain. *SNS Group*

Major milestone: The 50th anniversary of Barcelona is a chance to reflect on all we achieved together in 1972 and the impact it had on the lives of all who played their part. I'm pictured here in 2021 at Tom Miller's launch for his book Barcelona. *Glasgow Times*

Away days: Travelling home and abroad with the Dave Smith Loyal Fraserburgh RSC has been a pleasure. This picture was taken in Amsterdam on one of our many trips to watch the current team in Europe. Pictured with me are (from left): Richard Shaw, Kenny Brown, Ritchie Reid, Ian McLean, Billy Paterson, James Gibb and Martin Noble.

Match ready: My good friend Dave Hamilton and I have travelled the length and breadth of the country following Rangers.

Career on canvas: This wonderful montage was commissioned by the Dave Smith Loyal Fraserburgh RSC and painted by the excellent artist Helen Runciman. My copy was presented at Argyll House.

For the collection: A new commemorative badge has been created by the Dave Smith Loyal Fraserburgh RSC to mark the 50th anniversary.

Never too old: In action during a charity match at Ibrox in 2016 – the last time I played at my old stomping ground, at the grand old age of 72!

Family united: Sheila and I are incredibly proud of our family. Pictured, clockwise from left, are: Grandsons Zak and Tom, son-in-law Pascal, Sheila, Melanie, Paul, daughter-in-law Coral, granddaughters Zara and Mia, grandson Finlay, me and Amanda.

Special occasion: Pictured with my brother Doug and his wife May at my daughter Melanie's wedding.

Through the generations: I had the chance to run out at Ibrox with my grandson Finlay back in 2007 and he got a brilliant reception from the crowd when he scored at the Copland Road end – he's taller than me now and still wears the colours with pride!

VIP visit: With my grandsons Zak and Tom – Melanie and Pascal's boys – in the Ibrox trophy room during a visit to Scotland from their home in California.

Growing up fast: Pictured with my grandchildren Finlay, Mia and Zara – Paul and Coral's children - back in 2015. Our dogs Ollie and Millie were doing their best to get in on the photo.

a golfer marking distances. Whenever I had the chance, whether in advance of a game or in the warm-up, I'd hit long diagonals from corner to corner to get my range.

The Sunday night was a case of settling in at the hotel, resting up after the flight and getting some light food.

If you visited the Gran Hotel Rey Don Jaime now I don't think you would recognise it as the same area, it's a bit better connected now the town has grown up around it. The hotel has changed too – familiar in parts from the outside, but a touch more luxurious inside than I remember it from the 1970s!

Tucked away in the countryside, it had a dubious claim to fame. Just a few weeks before we arrived, the Hollywood film star George Sanders took his own life while staying at the hotel, leaving a note to say he was 'bored' and 'had lived enough'. It was a bizarre piece of news to introduce us to our base for the trip, but it was obviously still fresh in the minds of the staff and locals.

Back then there was nothing around us at all. If we went for a walk we didn't see a soul. I guess that's why it was chosen – away from distractions. There were racquetball courts which we would have loved to try out, but anything more than a game of dominoes by the pool was strictly off limits.

The following day we headed to the Sarria Stadium, home to Espanyol at that time, for the first of our sessions in Spain.

John Greig and Colin Jackson were both still carrying those injuries which had been a concern in the warm-up games, so it was a chance for the manager to keep an eye on them and get a feel for whether they were ready.

Dynamo had a couple of injury worries themselves, the striker Vladimir Koslov the most prominent. The Scottish media had been out to their hotel on the outskirts of the city, and the team news was the focus in the days leading up to the game.

In our squad, for those pushing for a place in the team the

Sarria workout was one of the last chances to persuade the manager that they deserved that shirt.

Despite the change of surroundings and the blazing sunshine, there was no change to our usual routine. Training was sharp and lively, but we did the work we would normally do, and there was certainly no sense of fear about the Russians, or any special plans being laid.

Although we were being wrapped in cotton wool off the training pitch, a fresh injury to Colin Jackson during the first of our training stints was the first bit of negativity to hit the preparations. It was impossible not to feel for Bomber, who did damage to his ankle in one of our training games in Spain. It wasn't the knock he had been nursing before we flew out, but a different injury.

He had been desperate to play and tried right up to the 11th hour to prove his fitness, but I think in his heart of hearts knew it was a losing battle.

That paved the way for Derek Johnstone's place to be confirmed in the defence. With John winning his fitness battle it left one name to be picked from Andy Penman, Alfie Conn and Derek Parlane for the creative spot in midfield.

That was a decision for another day – the emphasis early in the week was on keeping us occupied and relaxed, with a trip out on the Monday night to watch England take on West Germany in the final of the European under-18 championship. They won 2-0, so there were a couple of British success stories in Barcelona that week. It's fair to say one is celebrated more than the other.

TEN

'THIS WAS OUR TIME AND OUR CHANCE TO BE HEROES'

MAY 24. GAME DAY. The biggest match in the club's history – and if you wanted to see it, you had to be there.

The SFA had made sure of that by ruling it couldn't be broadcast live in Scotland because of the national side's match against Wales that night. How ludicrous does that sound now? The biggest one-off game in the club's history and it was a TV blackout. Even the highlights had to be held back until after 11pm because of SFA rules, which initially meant it couldn't be screened at all, with the BBC and STV both giving it a belated showing after the club had made a special request.

That gives a little glimpse into the way our game was run, and you could argue not an awful lot has changed in terms of attitudes at the top of Scottish football. Self-interest and petty rivalries, as Rangers have found out to their cost, are never far from the surface.

Even if it had been broadcast on every channel simultaneously, I don't think anything would have stopped the tens of thousands who made the trip to Spain.

Every travel agent in the city – and some far beyond – seemed to be offering packages. By boat, bus, trains, planes and automobiles there was a clamour to be part of something special.

Ticket sales were being run through the SFA, as our home association, rather than the club, and they were inundated with requests.

There wasn't the usual pressure when it came to tickets. With a capacity of 90,000 or so, the Nou Camp could swallow up as many as could afford to make the trip – and with the Russian borders closed for the Dynamo supporters, there would be no opposition supporters in Spain.

The official Russian party was limited to just 25 – that's players, coaches and officials. They had arrived via Paris, where they had to stop to collect visas, and flew in the same day as us.

This was still a time when the Soviet state restricted any travel abroad for individuals without special dispensation. Once they were out it was very much a short-term leave. Refusal to return was treated as treason, with imprisonment or, in extreme cases, the death penalty held as the deterrent. It put any grumbles we might have had into perspective.

That was one of the quirks of the final and, although it made sure everyone who could get to Barcelona was able to get into the ground, in so many ways it wasn't helpful.

We were a group who thrived on the big occasions – as the two matches against Bayern had shown – and we fed off the energy of the crowd. Don't get me wrong, the atmosphere in Barcelona was fantastic because of the numbers who made the trip, but having a bit of needle between the opposing groups on the terraces as well as on the pitch always added extra spice.

The attendance figure of more than 35,000 was made up almost entirely of Rangers supporters, save for that tiny official party from Moscow and the usual UEFA dignitaries.

That was a record-breaking travelling support for a European final, bearing in mind foreign travel was very much a luxury.

For most fans it meant parting with a big chunk of their wages to join the adventure, and that sacrifice wasn't lost on the squad.

Driving up to the stadium on the night of the match, it hit home how well backed we would be – it was a sea of red, white and blue around the ground, and as it began to fill with Rangers fans the atmosphere was building.

By then we were fed and watered, sticking to the usual routine we had of a pre-match meal a couple of hours before kick-off. Some liked to eat well but for me a cup of tea was all I really wanted or needed.

A dressing room can be a strange place before any match, not least one of that significance. There's a void to be filled between arriving and getting started. You take far longer to do everything, just to try and kill time. Fixing your kit, getting stripped, massages, stretching – anything to keep busy when all you want to do is get out and play.

We had a real mix in terms of how the tension before a game was handled. John Greig was the noisy one. He kept things bubbling away on the bus and around the ground, until it was time to get the game face on. Then you knew he meant business.

Willie Johnston could be a bundle of nerves at times – pacing and, for him, quiet. A few pre-match cigarettes, hidden away in the toilets, sometimes helped to settle him! Then Bud would go out and destroy teams, full of confidence and showboating.

Me? I don't think I ever really changed. Once I'd settled into a squad and people got to know me, I opened up and liked a laugh. Pre-match I was pretty laid back, some probably thought a bit too laid back.

It took me a while after making the move from Aberdeen to feel like I belonged. I felt like I had to prove myself before I started to come out of my shell. By '72 that was all behind me.

The preparation was done in the build-up to the game, back home in Glasgow and then in the couple of days on the training field in Barcelona.

The difficulties with broadcast and media weren't reserved for home soil though. The Iron Curtain meant getting any tapes or reports on Dynamo was practically impossible for the manager and his staff.

Although we had by chance played them just 12 months previously in a pre-season friendly at Ibrox, when Derek Johnstone had scored the only goal of the game, there was the feeling that it was a very different animal we were about to face.

Their results in the run-up to the final were excellent – they had navigated a passage past Olympiacos, the Turkish side Eskisehirspor, Red Star Belgrade and the Berlin outfit BFC Dynamo. An easier route than our own for certain, but some very decent sides on that hit list.

When you look at the clubs who had set out in the first round hoping to get their hands on the silverware, it was a great achievement to reach the final. Liverpool and Chelsea, Barcelona and Steaua Bucharest, Austria Vienna and Sparta Rotterdam were among them.

Lev Yashin had retired from playing the previous year and seemed destined to continue his success with Dynamo after moving upstairs. It was never quite clear what his role was – administrator, coach, poster boy?

He was as cool and calm as he had been on the pitch, and his presence around the Dynamo squad was obviously a massive confidence boost for them. He was one of the game's true superstars, and it was his side that stood between us and the trophy.

We were given as thorough a briefing as we could get on the likely 11, including mapping out where the biggest threats would come from.

Anatoli Kozhemyakin, a young striker, and Gennady Yevryuzhikhin, an experienced World Cup winger with speed to burn and a cupboard full of Russian caps, were among them – but Yozhef Sabo in midfield, as has been well covered over the years, was another who was earmarked for close attention. He was viewed as a key man and a leader at the heart of the Dynamo team, but there were others. The captain Victor Anichkin, a defender who was a mainstay for his national side, and the winger Vladimir Eshtrekov, a bag of tricks, were the other notable names.

The connection between the clubs, stretching back to the famous match in the 1940s, added an extra dimension to the final and there was a mutual respect. Dynamo had been league winners in Russia in the 1960s and were aiming to regain that place as top dogs.

Waddell did get a chance to watch them in the flesh, in the week leading up to the final, and he came back with his usual comprehensive dossier.

He prepared us for what he expected to be an open and attacking game, with the scouting mission highlighting well-organised but relatively free-flowing opposition. We knew they would be strong, quick and resilient but had anticipated it would be a stuffy game, with Russian teams of that era renowned for structure and tenacity rather than flair.

Instead, the clear message was that a 0-0 was unlikely. Not for the first time, the pre-match analysis proved to be on the money. We had also been told to be aware the Spanish referee Sergio Gonella wasn't afraid to reach for his cards – so hard but fair was the mantra. For those who liked to tackle at least, so not a concern for me!

After the confusion in Lisbon, the club had been at pains to clarify what the permutations were if it wasn't settled in 90 minutes. A replay, two days later, was pencilled in and only then would it go to extra time and penalties if there was no winner. Settling it at the first attempt was everyone's preferred option.

As well prepared as we always were, once you've done the homework and landed on the approach, it has to be put to the back of your mind. For me, any Rangers team, no matter who they're playing against, should be setting out to impose themselves on the game and aiming to dictate the pace.

In Barcelona we did that. From that first tackle by John on Sabo to the first dribble from Bud and my first break forward with the ball, it was about giving Dynamo something to think about.

Nothing that we heard really changed our approach. Although we were expecting them to come at us, there was still an emphasis on us to be the attacking force and find the key to unlock Dynamo. Against Bayern in the semi-final, we knew we would be forced to defend for periods of both legs, but over 90 minutes at the Nou Camp the onus was on us to take the game to the Russians. We considered ourselves favourites and had to play that way.

By the time the team bus snaked its way from our hotel up in the hills at Castelldefels to the Nou Camp, right in the heart of the city, we were as ready as we would ever be.

The starting 11 had been announced – the final part of the jigsaw slotted in with Alfie Conn getting the nod for that last precious place. Alfie was a prodigious young talent, just turned 20 when he lined up that night, and he had all the ability in the world – not to mention the confidence and swagger you need as a playmaker.

The handwritten note from the manager, laying out his possible line-up, can still be seen in the trophy room. At No. 8 you can make out Penman, Conn, Parlane – showing how close a call it was for him. All three were in the running right up to the wire, and it was Alfie who got the nod. He'd been on good form in the warm-up games and lively in training, pushing himself to the head of the queue.

It hurts me, I think it hurts us all in fact, that some sections of the support haven't been able to forgive Alfie for signing for Celtic in 1977. As he's said himself on many occasions, he was a professional who took the best offer on the table at that time. Had Rangers been an option, he would have been back at Ibrox like a shot I'm sure – just as we all would have done if the call had come. It didn't for Alfie, and he landed at Parkhead.

I know it's easy to say, but the Old Firm rivalry shouldn't detract from the service he gave to the club and the part he played that night in Barcelona. He is a Rangers legend.

With the team named before we reached the Nou Camp, the manager's part was peripheral really. Team talks pre-match were brief and to the point – a rallying call more than anything. I'd be lying if I said I could remember anything that was shared in the dressing room before we left – it's just noise at that stage.

We didn't need anyone to tell us that this was our time and our chance to be heroes.

It took us two attempts at coming out for the kick-off. At the first, we were told to turn back and go back inside because of supporters on the pitch. It was an early sign of the problems there would be, with so few police on duty to keep a lively support in check.

The Nou Camp is a place that's in all of our hearts. There's a slight contradiction in that it's the stadium of 1972 that means so much to me, the modern-day equivalent is more than a little bit different.

Yes it's the same ground and yes it's the same location. So much has changed over the years that it's difficult to picture yourself on that pitch.

The one and only time I've been back was in the winter of 2007 when we were guests at the Barcelona v. Rangers tie in the

Champions League. It wasn't a memorable night on the pitch as far as the travelling supporters were concerned, but it certainly sticks in my mind.

Barça ran out 2-0 winners with goals from Thierry Henry and a certain Lionel Messi. The goalscorers alone underlined the impossible task that night. Behind them they had Andrés Iniesta and Xavi, with Carles Puyol and Lilian Thuram at the back. From a purist's perspective, it was fascinating to see them at work in their own environment in front of more than 85,000 fans. When you consider the return leg at Ibrox ended 0-0 there was no shame in the result in Spain.

We had the opportunity to get onto the pitch for photos and to soak up the atmosphere from pitch level, but it was the company not the venue that brought the real sense of nostalgia.

To put it in context, when we played there it was a relatively new ground, opened just 15 years earlier. By all accounts the construction had just about bankrupted Barcelona, so the financial issues we read about today aren't altogether unheard of.

It was originally intended to have a capacity of 150,000, but they settled for a more modest 93,000 for the final design. My memory of it is as a big concrete dish. Like so many buildings of that era, it certainly wasn't a thing of beauty or tradition like we had with the Main Stand at Ibrox.

You still had the large covered section that there is today, shielding the expensive seats, but the majority was open to the summer sky as it still is. The floodlights were low, rather than pylons like we were used to, and it felt like a wall of light when you came out of the tunnel for the first time.

It was a mix of standing and seating, with the curved stands wrapping right round the pitch like you see today. That meant there was a big track area around the pitch, so you felt distant from the crowd – at least while they were in the stands!

I've played at plenty of grounds like that, the old Hampden

being a case in point, and I don't think you'd find a single player who prefers it that way. You want the connection you get with the crowd when they're right on top of you. Mind you, a track has its benefits if things aren't going to plan and you can't hear the comments coming your way.

It was two tiers back then, so didn't tower over you in quite the same way as it does today. That was probably the biggest difference I noticed when we were back on the park in 2007 – the sheer height is incredible.

From the outside there are still very familiar parts, although a lot more glass and a more polished feel now. We definitely didn't have the huge scoreboards, just flags flying overhead.

A third tier was added in the 1980s to take the capacity up to 115,000 at one point, and in the 1990s the pitch was lowered to squeeze in more seats. The removal of standing areas chopped the maximum it can hold down to just below 100,000, and, when it's packed and in full flow, it's a wonderful place to watch a game.

While the stadium has got bigger, the pitch has actually shrunk to fit with current UEFA guidelines. It was, at one stage, one of the longest and widest parks in the world and for '72 it certainly felt that way with vast open spaces which were perfect for the way we liked to play. There were willing runners in Steiny and Bud just waiting to get in behind.

I have to say, aside from Ibrox, obviously, it's the stadium that must be the best I've ever played in. There were some incredible arenas in America, for example, but the history and everything that goes with the Nou Camp makes it a standout.

It felt like you had walked a marathon just to get to the dressing rooms because of the size of the place. Although it wasn't particularly ornate or grand, mainly because it was so new and was all painted brick and wooden panelling, the big-club feel was impossible to miss. Even back then, Real Madrid and

Barça were competing on and off the park to be the biggest and best, and the stadiums reflected that.

Not that it would have mattered where we were. The celebrations would have been the same at the Nou Camp or Gayfield. Once the trophy arrived it was all a bit of a blur.

You enter the arena from underground, gladiator style. As you come up stairs that lead pitchside, you catch sight of the vast ground that it is. You get a bit of everything: the terraces, the lights, the sky beyond.

It's not so much about what you see though, it's about what you hear. It may not have been full, far from it, but with the sound the travelling supporters made you would never have guessed it. When that noise hits you as you run out, you feel your heart pounding in your chest.

What follows from there is the most difficult sensation to explain. For me, what hit when I crossed the white line was a sense of calm. I didn't play angry, I didn't get excitable. It was complete focus on the game in hand.

I also didn't get too carried away in the moment. If we scored, you wouldn't find me running the length of the pitch to celebrate with the forwards. At that moment, it's all about keeping your concentration and getting set. If you let your emotions take over, positive or negative, that's when you become vulnerable.

My whole game was built on being able to read the game, and as soon as you lose control or get wrapped up in anything else around you then you're a step behind.

The tempo was set, as has been well recorded, with that crunching challenge by John on Sabo in the opening seconds. Then another sharp tackle by Alex MacDonald in the midfield. If they didn't know it before, the Russians understood it wasn't going to be an easy night.

In any game you want an early touch and a chance to settle into the match, and I got that. The first pass, drilled low into the feet of Colin Stein, came off, and from there you just want more and more of the ball – and that night I got it. There was time and space, opportunities for me to arrow long diagonals left to Bud and into the channels for Steiny. There was even a collector's item of a shot from 30 yards. I didn't score many of those and that didn't change with that one!

The Russians chose not to press, sitting deep and defending in numbers, so I was free to pick the ball up from Peter McCloy on the edge of the box and drive forward at will. Derek Johnstone was able to pick his moments too, and the two of us had as much of a role to play going forward as we did defending, certainly in the first half. DJ, in fairness, was snapping into tackles all over the park too and never missed a beat.

We dominated possession in the early stages, and that gave us the belief to go on and push for goals. When the first one came, in the 23rd minute, it felt like the door had opened.

There was as good a chance just a couple of minutes earlier, when I darted forward and slipped the ball into Alex MacDonald inside the box – only for a last-gasp tackle to cut out the shot.

We kept probing, and it was another break forward that brought the breakthrough. This time I went long, looping a pass to Colin Stein in the inside-right position, and he brushed off the defenders to finish with the style which we were all so accustomed to. He was the perfect No. 9 and a joy to play behind – he made unselfish runs all game long, with the power and pace to bully defenders, and when they came off he had the touch and guile to make it pay.

A one-goal cushion was never going to be enough – we were experienced enough in Europe to know there would be twists and turns to come. We kept pushing and eventually got the reward five minutes before half-time.

A poor clearance from Dynamo landed at my feet and left me with a gap to push forward into. I didn't spend too much time on the right wing in a career spanning two decades, but it paid off on this occasion. A step-over, a cut back onto my left foot and an inswinging cross which was met beautifully by Bud inside the box. He'd made a brilliant blindside run and got up so well to place a header right in the bottom-left corner. No keeper on earth was saving that.

He and Steiny did an incredible amount of the spadework in that campaign, the ugly side of being a glamorous forward. They hassled and harried, showed for the ball all over the park and took the blows that came their way. That typified the spirit we had, all for one. If two men deserved to score in the final it was them.

You go in two goals ahead at half-time thinking the job's just about done and there isn't much to be said or anything to be changed at the break. Keep doing the things we were doing, and the trophy was coming back home with us.

When the third went in, just four minutes into the second half, we were in dreamland. Peter's long high kick caught the Russian defence flat-footed, preoccupied with Steiny's challenge for the ball, and Bud raced in from the edge of the box to slot it past Vladimir Pilguy in the Moscow goal. It was another clinical finish. Peter's kicking isn't always given the credit it deserves. He could hit distances unlike any other goalkeeper I played with, but he had the accuracy to match.

At 3-0 up you think *game over*. The olé football came out – if you can't be a bit cocky when you're three ahead in a European final, when can you?

As it happens, we were a bit ahead of ourselves. Far from being dead and buried, they came back at us with a real determination.

Maybe not surprisingly we began to tire. We had John carrying an injury and the rest of us hadn't played competitively for weeks, and they had fresh legs that made an impact. Whereas we would only make substitutions if there were injuries, they brought on Vladimir Eshtrekov and Mikhail Gershkovich either side of the hour mark and it made, for the neutrals at least, for an entertaining last half hour.

We would quite happily have taken a dull final 30.

Eshtrekov – wearing what proved to be lucky 13 – scored with just about his first touch of the ball. It was all too easy in truth. They nicked the ball on the right side, outside the box, and broke forward to cross for a tap-in.

We didn't set out to defend deep and kept pushing for openings, but there's no doubt Dynamo put us under the type of pressure they hadn't come close to matching in the first half. That said, we created plenty of chances of our own – even in the dying minutes Steiny could have had a second had it not been for a good save. Three would just have been greedy though.

After that came the real scare, with the Russians getting their second goal back. A neat little one-two on the edge of the box and a clipped shot over Peter to make it 3-2.

Three minutes left on the clock. Three minutes that felt like a lifetime, not helped by the delay to clear the pitch after premature celebrations brought the crowds flooding on.

Personally, I didn't for a second in that game feel like we were in danger. I can't speak for anyone else, and you could point to the mistakes we made as a team to let them back in as signs of nervousness creeping into our play, but the scoreline flattered Dynamo. To go three goals ahead in a European final is pretty remarkable, they're usually cagey affairs, and it reflected the control we had for the majority of the match.

Don't get me wrong, they were a good side. Bayern, given everything they went on to achieve, were the best team we overcame on that run, but I do believe the Russians were a match for them that season. They had technical ability and good individual players, they had a discipline and strength about them too.

I'm not a big believer in 'What if?' – but can you imagine if we had lost from 3-0 up? I don't think any of us would ever have got over that. I can't picture the reception we would have got back home if that had unfolded!

Not being nervous on the pitch is one thing, but I would imagine if you looked over to the dugout the faces of Waddell and Wallace might have told a different story. It's completely different when you're on the park and can influence a match. For all those on the touchline, and the supporters on the terraces, I suppose it would have felt like we were going through the wringer.

Despite the tension and all the drama, there was too much to lose for us to let it slip after everything we had put in. We rode the storm and came through it as European Cup Winners' Cup winners. Mission accomplished.

ELEVEN

'THE CALM AFTER THE STORM'

IT'S VERY DIFFICULT to put into words the sense of relief and joy that followed the final whistle. After the bedlam on the pitch, I can't even remember getting away from the crowds and back to the relative calm in the dressing rooms below. It was all just a blur. You go into autopilot as all of the emotions come crashing together.

What I do recall is that's when the party started, with the beer and champagne flowing and the songs being belted out from the giant baths deep in the Nou Camp.

On one side of the room it was bouncing, on the other there were some taking a moment to try and come to terms with what we had achieved together. There were a few tears shed over the course of the next 24 hours, not just players but the manager and coaching staff too were caught up in it all.

The photographs from the aftermath paint the picture so well. It was a team together in the moment, everyone sharing something we had never experienced before and, although we didn't know it at the time, one we wouldn't experience again.

When the initial rush passes and the noise subsides, it's then that the enormity hits you and there's a moment or two to catch a breath. The calm after the storm.

Then the second wind hits. The coach trip from the stadium to our hotel wasn't short, but it flew past. By the time we navigated our way clear of the ground, where it was still busy outside, and through the city it was close to an hour.

As we zig-zagged our way through Barcelona we passed plenty of coaches full of Rangers supporters, who got a glimpse of the trophy that was being passed around our bus.

When we got back to the hotel our wives had arrived too for the party, and it was a fantastic atmosphere. There were impromptu speeches by the manager, and chairman John Lawrence, and there was emotion in both of those.

It was rare for Lawrence to address the players, but we knew how much it meant to the board on so many different levels. Firstly, they were supporters who had the club in their blood. Secondly, they were astute businessmen who could appreciate what the first European success would do for revenue through the gates and the social club primarily.

The plan after the game, or so we thought, was for the group to split up between the two hotels and for the couples to room together instead of having the wives at one place and the squad at another. The manager thought otherwise. He wanted the team to stay together, and after the party finished the bus took the visitors away.

John Greig and I sat up by the pool long into the morning, guarding the cup between us before taking it away back up to our room when we eventually caught a couple of hours' sleep. We woke to find a dent in the side of it that had to be repaired back in Glasgow. It had obviously taken a tumble, presumably along with one or both of us, at some point the night before.

We were fortunate to have a leisurely start the next day, with an afternoon flight out of Barcelona and back to Prestwick.

The press were with us and the photos on the runway tell their own story. Sunshine, smiling faces and not a care in the world.

Before a ball had been kicked, the plans were already in place for the victory parade – a sign of the logistics involved and the need to work with the police and authorities to manage the crowds rather than overconfidence.

We knew that if we did collect the trophy we would be coming back to Ibrox to give the supporters at home their first proper sight of the cup.

We landed back at Prestwick in the early evening and travelled straight to the ground, from the sunshine of the Costas straight into the worst of the west-coast weather.

The Lord Provost John Mains had travelled down to meet us as we arrived, a nice touch and an indication of the pride the city, or half of it at least, was taking in what we'd delivered for Glasgow.

The torrential rain made it all the more impressive that 25,000 supporters turned out at less than a day's notice to join in the celebrations. Given there was about the same number making their way back from Spain, in various states and by various means, it was a fantastic reception.

We travelled in the team coach from the airport to the stadium and gathered in the ground, waiting for the crowds to filter in, before heading out of the tunnel. The supporters in that night raised the roof – it was an incredible reception.

I'm not entirely sure who had enlisted the now famous coal truck for the lap of honour, but it did the trick. Not quite an open-top bus parade, but it didn't matter. We did a couple of laps of the stadium, with the noise not dropping for a second, and it was incredible looking out and seeing supporters who, judging by the sombreros, had been in the crowds at the Nou Camp cheering us on there too.

One of the best parts of getting back to Ibrox was being able to share the celebrations with all those who were the lifeblood of the club, not just the supporters but the staff too.

The saying that nobody is bigger than the club is so true at Rangers. Then, just like now, the work that goes on behind the scenes to keep the machine running is incredible and so much of it goes unseen and probably under-appreciated outside of Ibrox.

Within the stadium itself, I think there was, and I'm sure still is, a real understanding of all the moving parts which fit together.

The players are the ones who get the plaudits when things are going well, but that's just the tip of the iceberg.

I've mentioned at various stages the support we had from the coaching staff on the road to Barcelona, including Joe Craven and Stan Anderson as well as Willie Thornton in his role on the backroom staff.

The physio Tommy Craig's attention to detail and Dr Donald Cruickshank's care also go without saying, but there was an army of people away from the playing side who did a power of work to look after us.

Lizzie Love, who had been at Ibrox for a long time before I arrived and whose role grew and grew over the years, was a case in point. She was responsible for keeping the stadium shipshape but also cooked for us as well as the directors and other officials plus generally running the inside of the stadium as a mother figure for the younger boys in particular. There was Maggie Lindsay in the laundry, responsible for the countless hampers of kit we got through – the emphasis at Rangers on and off the park was looking sharp, the best kit and always a shirt and tie for coming to 'work'. Could you really call it work?

Together with his team, Davie Marshall's domain was the outside, as head groundsman, and it was a relentless task given the number of games we were ploughing through at the peak times. Ibrox has never been the easiest park to tend to. I've always been told the water table's high because of the proximity to the Clyde, but we prided ourselves on having one of the best pitches in the game. The crew also looked after the stand and terraces, so put in hard shifts. There were the painters and handymen too, all working together to keep the ground in order.

On matchdays there were the turnstile operators, the programme sellers, first-aid volunteers – the list goes on and on.

Bobby Moffat, the face of Rangers in so many ways, is one who gets special mention. Bobby, as doorman, had been involved with the club as man and boy – as far back as when he was Bill Struth's driver. Willie Webb, a former referee, worked the entrance on match days too in his role as commissionaire, always immaculately turned out, and his experience of keeping players in check undoubtedly helped him maintain order when managing the crowds.

Coming in that entrance at Ibrox still gives me goosebumps, seeing the marble staircase and the history of the place around every corner. To this day, I always wear a collar and tie to the ground.

But it's always been about the people rather than the bricks and mortar. From the welcome of the doorman to the hospitality of the directors, that's what has always made it more than just another football club.

They deserved as much credit as anyone on the playing side, and I know they took as much pride as we did in the days, weeks and months that followed.

The celebrations went on long into the summer, culminating in a banquet in the City Chambers on 18 September, hosted by the new Lord Provost William Gray. There's not too much logic to the things you keep and the things you throw away, but I've still got the menu from that night – complete with scribbles from my daughter Amanda, who must have got hold of it for some handwriting practice!

A toast to the Queen was followed by a formal welcome from the Lord Provost, with speeches by the chairman John Lawrence and, as he was by then, general manager Willie Waddell. There was entertainment from the opera singer Helen MacArthur and a vote of thanks by James Aitken, president of the Scottish Football League, before a rousing rendition of 'Auld Lang Syne'. I'd love to say I remember it all – but it turns out a near 50-year-old scribbled-on memento has its uses. I knew it would come in handy one day.

For completeness, the menu consisted of grapefruit and melon cocktail followed by celery soup, baked rainbow trout and then a mixed grill with roast potatoes, buttered mushrooms, creamed potatoes and asparagus tips. The desert was 'Rangers Delight' – and no, I've got no idea what that was!

It was all washed down with Château de la Tour Clos-Vougeot (1967), Piesporter Goldtröpfchen (1970) and then Courvoisier cognac and Drambuie. Just in case you fancy recreating that celebratory meal and raising a glass to a job well done.

I don't have many other pieces of merchandise or mementoes from Barcelona as such – other than the medal of course, which I guess is the one that matters most.

There had been a programme for the 1967 final but not for the one in '72. As players we obviously didn't have tickets or passes of any sort, and I don't remember us ever handling our own plane boarding cards and the likes either – we just turned up and followed instructions!

There was the matador poster dotted around the city, but we didn't get copies of that ourselves. I know some supporters got their hands on the originals and there are reproductions doing the rounds too, as well as the one in the trophy room at Ibrox – complete with the incorrect spelling of Willie Johnston's name (with an E on the end). There have even been replicas of the medals produced as keyrings, which are a very good likeness of the real thing.

Barcelona merchandise has become relatively big business in more recent times, not for the players I hasten to add! It isn't uncommon to have semi-professional autograph hunters pitching up at the house looking for a signature on a shirt, a programme or photo, and I've never said no.

If you have a quick search online you could throw up any number of items for sale from all sorts of collectors across the country and beyond. Verifying the authenticity is always the important thing; I'd hate to think of any Rangers supporters being tempted to part with money for anything that isn't quite what it seems.

Of course, Club 72 at the stadium is maybe the most obvious branding exercise there has been and a very popular one at that.

Maybe we should have had agents to thrash out royalty deals and image rights, but I don't think any of us are wired that way. Signed shirts and pictures, those keyrings and posters, commemorative whisky and everything else in-between have been produced over the years. We have had benefits from some, but it has never been about pounds and pence for the squad.

I do have some of the commemorative magazines from after the final, but at the time you don't give a second's thought to that type of thing or what you might like to keep to look back on 50 years down the line.

What I am very lucky to have are cases full of scrapbooks, boxes of programmes, football magazines and assorted other reminders of that time. I would love to say that I collated and curated those, but it was my mum and dad who did all of that.

We weren't really aware of it at the time, but they must have been going out every morning and religiously scouring every paper for mentions of Doug, Hughie and me. Each one was clipped out and pasted into different volumes, from the early 1960s right through to the late 1970s.

It's quite the piece of work and a good indication of the pride they took in the achievements of their boys and what we were doing at 'work'. It's funny, the cuttings they kept are all positive – I don't recall seeing anything about the bad games! Maybe we never had those though.

Of course, we knew that at the time but it's when you look back at the little things, like a two-line cutting carefully snipped from the paper, that you appreciate how much it meant to them to see us living out our dreams. There was another member of the Smith clan who featured quite regularly in that coverage, with Caesar our boxer dog a popular prop for the photographers. We had another boxer, Brandy, after him and they were the real favourite sons!

The other relics alongside the dusty newspaper cuttings are piles and piles of telegrams, all neatly still in their envelopes. I've got everything from notifications of call-ups for international duty to the notes of congratulations we got at our wedding. When you saw the telegram boy arriving you knew something important, or at least interesting, was about to be imparted – it was like a human equivalent of the WhatsApp icon popping up on your phone!

If anything illustrates how much has changed in the past 50 years it's exactly that. If someone wanted to get in touch or tell you something they had to physically track you down, and it meant you lived in your own bubble for the large part.

When we were downstairs in the Nou Camp celebrating, it was just those of us in the room, nobody from the outside could touch us, and we were living it all in the moment rather than through what was happening on social media or phone screens.

For me that's a huge positive – we soaked all of it up there and then, rather than seeing it through our camera screens like you see so often with celebrations on the pitch and behind the scenes today. Where I am envious is of the footage and pictures our modern-day counterparts will have to look back on. What I wouldn't give to have my own videos from the dressing room in the Nou Camp when we came back in, to be able to relive just a couple of minutes of that rush of celebration.

Sitting down to write this book, it's incredible how much you remember – but also how much you forget. Reading cuttings, watching back newsreels and match highlights jogs the memory to a certain extent, but it's the less formal bits that it would be brilliant to have a record of. We didn't even take that many photos. I don't think any of us had a camera with us either around the hotel before and after the match or when we were at the stadium. We didn't feel like we needed to because we had photographers with us every step of the way, but that means all that really survives are the official archives rather than anything more personal.

What we won't ever forget is the significance of the win.

It was one team per country, so it was still European knock-out football in its purest form. The competition was born in 1960. Rangers historians won't need reminding that the inaugural tournament held good and bad memories, with the high of making the final against the low of losing out over two legs to Fiorentina in 1961.

For the club to have played in three finals is no mean feat. Only AC Milan, Arsenal and Atletico Madrid did likewise. Barcelona, with six final appearances, and Anderlecht, with four, are the only clubs who bettered it.

The success of the early tournaments led to a number of nations introducing domestic cup competitions just to gain entry to it. By the late 1960s every UEFA member had fallen into line and the European Cup Winners' Cup was going from strength to strength, leading to the 32-team line-up that we found ourselves in. Five rounds, nine matches and the trophy was yours. Simple!

In saying that, it's the one win that means everything. There are some huge names on that roll of honour alongside ours: Bayern Munich, Juventus, Manchester United, Ajax – the list goes on.

The fact it ran for 39 years is a good indication of the success of the format, and it was a shame to see the competition, and the trophy, confined to the history books when it was rolled into the UEFA Cup in 1999. In turn, both were replaced by the Europa League.

I've had the fortune to attend many Rangers games in the Champions League and the Europa League and I certainly wouldn't argue against the progress there's been in terms of building those brands and tournaments. More games through the introduction of the group stages, more broadcast and sponsorship revenue, more money through the gate. It all adds up to make commercial sense. Supporters have bought into it, and the big European nights at Ibrox are still a sight and sound to behold.

What I don't see as progress is the qualifying process and the hurdles that teams, particularly Scottish sides and Rangers in particular, have had to overcome in recent years. Round after round early in the season, when players are still getting up to speed, against opposition that it's difficult to get excited about. Improving the coefficient to avoid the perils of qualifying is the only way around it, and at least we're seeing movement in the right direction.

The names may have changed, and the trophies have grown in size, but a lot of the familiar patterns have stayed the same. English, Spanish, Italian and, to a lesser extent, German sides dominated the Cup Winners' Cup during its lifetime. The fact we didn't face a club from any of those countries in the final was a bit of a novelty.

It was the first European trophy taken back to Britain, with Tottenham beating Atletico Madrid 5-1 in Rotterdam in 1963. A double from the late Jimmy Greaves helped them on their way, having beaten Rangers in the earlier rounds.

Our own final was sandwiched between Chelsea's notable victory against Real Madrid in 1971 and AC Milan's narrow win over Leeds United in 1973. Both of those games were played in Greece, not quite on the same level as a trip to the Nou Camp and a bit of a quirk given the way the finals were shared out widely among UEFA host nations.

Chelsea had to do it the hard way, taken to a replay two days after the original game and in the same venue. Like us the following year, they were going for their first piece of European silverware, and they had the pedigree to do it. I had a vested interest, with my good pal Charlie Cooke a mainstay of that team, and it was brilliant to see him on the winning side. Charlie had the likes of Peter Bonetti, Ron 'Chopper' Harris, Alan Hudson and Peter Osgood for company, and it was a team very well equipped to play at that level.

In saying that, we felt our team was every bit as good, if not better, than any of the leading lights in England. Even half a century ago there was still a perception that Scottish football was not on the same level, but we played regularly enough against opposition from south of the border to know where we stood, and it was very much on even terms.

That Chelsea team, full of big-name stars with all the glitz and glamour of London's West End surrounding them, is a case in point.

We provided the opposition for the Ron Harris testimonial match in the winter of 1971, on the back of their European success, and ruined the party when Sandy Jardine scored the only goal of the game with a rasping long-range effort right at the end. In true testimonial style, Bonetti was playing outfield by that point, but, in Sandy's defence, there was a proper keeper in the shape of John Phillips to beat.

It wasn't just Sandy who hadn't read the script, with Willie Henderson giving Harris a torrid time and turning him inside out at every opportunity. Although technically a friendly, Willie Waddell was always quick to remind us that we were representing Rangers Football Club and that nothing short of a win was acceptable in any fixture.

The Chelsea manager Dave Sexton said he was surprised by just how good we were. We could turn it on in those exhibition matches, all the tricks and flicks would come out, and we did that night. Thousands of our own supporters travelled down and enjoyed their day out in London. There was no doubt about the pulling power of Rangers though – that's why we got invites to those type of games.

It was a bit of a surreal occasion – everyone from Richard Attenborough to Bernie Winters was there to meet the players afterwards. There was no sign of Schnorbitz.

We played English opposition fairly regularly during that period and they were always close encounters. We certainly won our share of them.

In the build-up to the 1971/72 season, we beat Everton 2-1 at Ibrox, with DJ scoring both, and won 1-0 against Spurs at home thanks to a goal from Bud. It was a sign of the way the team was coming together.

The win against Everton was a good barometer of our progress. From Joe Royle, Brian Labone, Howard Kendall and Alan Ball to Gordon West and Colin Harvey, they were full of top-class and international players.

I sat out the Everton and Spurs games, still on my way back from the broken leg, but being around those fixtures you got a good feel for the levels. Rangers would have been competing at the business end of the top flight.

When you bear in mind that Colin Stein and I had both turned down the chance to go to Goodison, it's a good indication of the way Rangers at that time could maintain a squad to match the championship-chasing English teams of that era.

We were at a similar level in continental terms too. Whereas Chelsea won their European Cup Winners' Cup final in 1971, Leeds fell short against Milan in 1973.

With their Scottish contingent of David Harvey, Peter

Lorimer, Frank Gray and Joe Jordan they were quite rightly a lauded side but fell at the last hurdle. There were accusations of match-fixing flying around at the time. Norman Hunter was red-carded in that one, although I'm not sure you could put that down to corruption! The Greek referee was banned for life on the back of an investigation, but bizarrely the result still stood. Even decades later, Leeds fans have been petitioning for it to be overturned. You have to admire their persistence.

When you look at the list of managers who have the European Cup Winners' Cup on their CV, Waddell is in pretty esteemed company. Giovanni Trapattoni, Johan Cruyff, Bobby Robson, Sven Göran Eriksson and not to mention two fellow Scots in Fergie and George Graham. It was a big prize won, more often than not, by big clubs and managers.

The top scorer list is like a who's who of world football – Gerd Müller, Gianluca Vialli, Hristo Stoichkov, Mario Kempes and a whole host of other top strikers.

Would we have swapped Colin Stein for any of them? Not a chance.

There were a few different variations of the trophy over the years; I believe the original is held by UEFA now. It did have a wooden base when we received it, but it wasn't attached so that was put to one side as the cup was passed around – filled and re-filled with beer and anything else we had to hand. The base was firmly fixed in later years and might have helped keep it on firm ground – we would certainly blame a design flaw for the dent it gained while in our care!

We could have been handed a battered tankard for all we cared. The most important thing was to put Rangers on the European roll of honour. That will be there for all time, no matter what shape or form the competitions take in the future.

TWELVE

'THE BIG OCCASIONS WERE THE MOTIVATION FOR ME'

ALONG WITH THE European Cup Winners' Cup medal, there are two other reminders of that 1971/72 season that are close to my heart.

The first is the bronze bust awarded to inductees to the Rangers Hall of Fame. That was presented in 2007, but it will forever be all about '72.

The second is a silver football on a wooden plinth. The prize for the Scottish Football Writers' Association Player of the Year. There's an assumption that the player of the year award came on the back of Barcelona, but in fact it was awarded weeks before the final.

The announcement was made long before the curtain fell on the season and the ceremony was on 9 May as we counted down to the final.

At that stage it was the only player of the year award nationally, before the Scottish PFA award was introduced, and it meant a lot to me to be recognised for what would have to be considered my best season.

Joe Harper was runner-up, with Kenny Dalglish also making the shortlist. Naturally I'd say the journalists made the right call.

When you look down the list of names that have been recognised, both before 1972 and since, it is very nice company to be in. From a Rangers perspective alone there's John Greig (1966 and 1976), Sandy Jardine (1975) who also won it while with Hearts (1986), Derek Johnstone (1978), Richard Gough (1989), Ally McCoist (1992), Andy Goram (1993), Mark Hateley (1994), Brian Laudrup (1995 and 1997), Paul Gascoigne (1996), Barry Ferguson (2000 and 2003), Carlos Cuellar (2008), David Weir (2010) and, most recently, Steven Davis (2021).

It's quite the Ibrox roll call and you could make not a bad 11 from that group of players. To be one of that number is something I do take pride in.

Martin Buchan, who won it the year prior to me before moving from Aberdeen to Manchester United, is the only other Aberdonian to have been honoured by the writers – another bit of trivia that puts into perspective the talent which was flowing through the city at that time.

There are only two Aberdeen-born players ever to have featured in a winning side in a European final by my reckoning.

Colin Jackson would of course have bolstered that number had it not been for his misfortune in Barcelona.

Denis Law would have been the first, had injury not kept him out of Manchester United's team for the European Cup final in 1968, so I took that honour in '72. Other than John Hewitt with Aberdeen in 1983, I can't think of another.

That said, I doubt too many in Aberdeen would be able to pick me out if you posed that as a quiz question. Once you move on to Rangers, achievements don't count in the eyes of most in my home city!

There are no complaints from me on that score. The recognition I've had matters far more to me than anything that hasn't come my way.

I also won around a dozen Rangers supporters' club player of the year awards in '72 – from Kilsyth to Maryhill and Coatbridge to Edinburgh, it was a busy period dashing from function to function. We headed north as a family to collect the award from the Caithness supporters' club in person, so reached all corners of the country on our mini tour. That flight to Wick, in a plane that felt like it was powered by a lawnmower engine, lives long in the memory.

There was even one from the Toronto Rangers Supporters' Club, although unfortunately for me that one was delivered to Glasgow by one of the visiting members on a trip back home. I've been fortunate to attend several North American Rangers Supporters Association conventions over the years, including in Canada, and the dedication of so many of the club's far-flung supporters is incredible. It's always an honour to be part of those events.

The Football Writers' dinner in 1972 was a brilliant occasion too. Harold Wilson, Leader of the Opposition by that stage between his two stints as Prime Minister, presented the award and the great and good of the game were there.

Willie Waddell was also one of the guest speakers, finding the time between trips out to cast an eye over the hotel and training facilities in Spain and his scouting mission in Russia.

Wilson, as the guest of honour, spoke well, as you would imagine, and obviously had done his homework, particularly when it came to what we were counting down to in Barcelona. He wasn't a stranger to Rangers mind you – Willie Henderson had actually been a guest at Downing Street while Wilson was in residence at No. 10. Willie always did know how to network!

To get that honour from the media was a real fillip. As I've touched upon, we regarded the sports writers as peers in many respects, and they had a significant place in the game. Mind you, they couldn't ignore me that season!

In all seriousness, it was humbling to be selected and to receive it in front of my contemporaries. I invited John Greig and Willie Mathieson as my guests on the night.

When the PFA Scotland Awards were introduced six years later, I was actually on the stage too – that was as Player of the Year in the Second Division with Berwick. Derek Johnstone won the main prize that night to make it a Rangers double! DJ won the writers' award that season too, fitting for a player who was so dominant at both ends of the pitch during his service to the club. I think people sometimes forget just how good Derek was, but nobody who played alongside him – or against him for that matter – would make that mistake.

Many years later, being inducted to the Rangers Hall of Fame was a similar feeling to the writers' award – quite awe-inspiring when you look at all of the names on the board at Ibrox, and just as importantly when you consider some of those who have yet to be added. To know that will be there long after I've paid my last visit to the stadium is a source of great pride.

The Player of the Year award and the Hall of Fame memento are among the few pieces of memorabilia from my playing career that we've ever had on display at home.

Both are a reflection of the years dedicated to the game. Both will be there against my name in the record books after I'm gone. In a team game, individual honours are few and far between, and anyone who tells you they don't mean something isn't being 100 per cent honest.

For all the years of graft I put in, both were on the back of that single season.

In fact, despite playing more than 300 games for Rangers and captaining the team, the Hall of Fame recognition is, it's fair to say, on the back of the success in Barcelona.

So, was it my best 90 minutes in a blue jersey? Not necessarily.

It's difficult to pick out just one. Barcelona, for obvious reasons, is certainly right up there. There were others though that were significant in different ways.

I was still a relatively young man when I made the move. As confident as I was with a ball at my feet in front of 70,000 supporters, I wasn't like that off the pitch. Once I get to know people I relax, but throw me into a room of strangers and I'm never at ease. After-dinner speaking isn't for me, that's for sure.

At Rangers I felt like I had to let my football do the talking. For that reason, the early games were important to me. Zaragoza in 1967, as I touched upon earlier, was a standout.

The other game that sticks in my mind wasn't a win, but it felt like it from a personal point of view. We played Celtic at Parkhead on a pitch that was like an ice rink in January 1970. It ended goalless, but we were the better team, and it was another of those days when it clicked for me – plenty struggled to get to grips with the conditions, but it felt like a stroll, and I got the man-of-the-match nod from the reporters. There are few better sounds than hearing the Rangers fans singing your name in an Old Firm game.

It didn't matter to me whether I was playing Celtic at Parkhead or Clydebank at Kilbowie, I always approached it the same way. Sometimes the tension of the big games played into my hands – the opposition didn't necessarily expect you to be trapping a high ball inside the six-yard box or knocking it through their legs on the penalty spot!

I maintain the two teams were closely matched during that period. Our undoing was struggling to take care of fixtures that should have been easy in comparison.

The atmosphere is everything you would imagine and the chance to play in that fixture was another tick in the box for me when it came to my move to Ibrox.

The big occasions were the motivation for me, not the rewards that came with being a Rangers player.

Were we well looked after? I would never argue otherwise. We certainly had a better lifestyle than the man in the street, but there was a certain prudence than ran through the club at that time.

On the back of Barcelona, Willie Johnston requested a transfer and a number of others from the starting 11 were involved in protracted contract talks – myself included. I had been on two-year contracts since signing in 1966, so the way it fell was renewal time coinciding with Barcelona and all that went with it.

The club was stung by Bud's request to move on. The manager was convinced he had been 'tapped up' by another club and lodged an official complaint, and they didn't want to lose others at a time when they were trying to build a league-winning team. Derek Johnstone was another who seemed to be on the brink, missing pre-season because of it, and despite the positive vibe among the players there was a definite tension within the club.

There were no agents. Contract talks were between the player and the manager, or general manager as Willie Waddell was by that stage. It could make it awkward in terms of managing relationships, but I was always pretty laid back and never difficult to deal with.

The issue at that stage was there was a feeling that we weren't being valued as we should have been. We knew the wages were better even at smaller clubs south of the border, so there was always a compromise on the side of the players. We were all willing to make that sacrifice because we understood the privilege we had in playing for Rangers, and all of those who were out of contract at that stage eventually settled on new terms.

None of us were holding out for a king's ransom; we weren't trying to live the lives of superstars.

The players' car park at Ibrox does give me a wry smile when I walk past today – Lamborghinis, Range Rovers as big as houses and every other high-end marque in-between. I don't grudge them it at all, but I think back to the Morris Marina I carried my European winner's medal back home in and have a little chuckle.

As Sheila likes to remind me, we kept a hammer in that less than trusty Marina to give the starter motor a nudge when it got stuck. That was the life of a 1970s star.

We had a little Italian coupe too – a Fiat 850. That was a little flying machine, or at least it was until somebody left the oil cap off and the engine seized. I'm still denying any knowledge of that.

I've never been a car buff, but there were some in the squad who liked to travel in style – Colin Jackson in his big black Mercedes and Tommy McLean's bright yellow Ford Capri stick in my mind. They certainly stood out in Govan. I read recently that Alfie Conn used his European bonus to buy a Cortina GT.

I've had my share of big Fords and a barge of a Jaguar (with an iffy fuel pump and alternator that meant you might have to get out and push or drive home in the dark, depending on which gave up first) over the years.

In truth I was happier in the Mini I drove when I first signed in 1966 (a replacement for the one I'd written off after passing my test) or the matching VW Beetles that Sheila and I bought not long after arriving in Glasgow.

The good people of the city may remember one of those Beetles, a bright orange one, which brought the south side to a standstill when Sheila abandoned it in the middle of Paisley Road West during a particularly fraught driving lesson. It turns out I'm not a great teacher – or she's not a great pupil! Given I took five (yes, five) attempts at passing my test, and Sheila sailed through at the first attempt, I'm in no place to take the high ground.

We actually went back to a Beetle, albeit the new version in recent years, and are now content zipping around in a little Fiat 500. That would look just the thing parked alongside the current squad's fleet!

It was a very different era and plenty of players had business interests outside of football. John Greig had his sports shop in Edinburgh, Willie Henderson had launched into the pub trade and had a hairdressing salon, and there were a few other enterprises springing up. Aside from being recruited as a columnist for the *Football Scot* when that magazine launched in 1970, I didn't branch out into anything else while I was playing and managing full time.

After arriving in Glasgow we rented a flat on Torbreck Street, a stone's throw from Ibrox and opposite Bellahouston Park, while we waited for our house on Harvie Avenue in Newton Mearns to be built.

We were away from family for the first time, and it was a big adventure for us both. So much is made of the gulf in wages between players of our generation and today, but we had a good lifestyle.

When we bought that first house I would have been on £60 per week or thereabouts, with bonuses topping that up along the way – although that dropped down by £10 if you weren't in the first team and £20 in the close season. That was probably about twice the average wage and around the mark a GP would have earned, so by no means were we badly looked after. I'd never argue that.

That was us in our early and mid-20s moving to a lovely new house in a fantastic area for a young family, kitted out with the best furniture and all the mod cons. A visit to the Ideal Home Show at Kelvingrove meant we even had a dishwasher. Who says we weren't living like rock stars in the 1960s?

It wasn't uncommon to have photoshoots at the house. We even featured in *Shoot!* magazine's 'At Home with the Stars' series.

We came down from Aberdeen and into a whole new world really. It's not as though we were country folk moving into the city from the sticks – Sheila and I had both grown up and lived practically right in the middle of Aberdeen from a young age, so we were used to that.

But Aberdeen and Glasgow were very different – not least in size. Glasgow back then was, if anything, bigger and busier than it is now. The exodus out of the centre and into the surrounding area and beyond hadn't quite taken full effect, although it was definitely starting. Aberdeen was tiny in comparison, long before the oil rush saw it spread north, south and west.

Although I had family in Glasgow it was a case of discovering it for ourselves, where to go and obviously where to live. You tend to get enclaves of footballers in different areas and suburbs; word of mouth has a big part to play in where you choose to set up home. A lot of those who stayed around Glasgow, from both sides of the Old Firm, had migrated out towards Newton Mearns, and that was where we settled after a brief time living in the city.

We loved it in Glasgow from the start. New places to see, new shops, restaurants and the buzz of being somewhere different. It was a time of transition when you look back at it – there were lots of buildings coming down, quite a lot of dereliction. For every building falling there was another springing up, and the reminders of the 1960s and 1970s are all around the city today. It felt like there was a lot of energy and buzz around at the time, although maybe everyone remembers their 20s like that.

The other big difference between Aberdeen and Glasgow wasn't so much in the surroundings but in the people. People Make Glasgow was a thing long before it was a slogan.

From day one we were welcomed with open arms and the warmth of the west coast is very different from the opposite side of the country. That's not to say Aberdeen's unfriendly, just an awful lot more reserved. That's reflected in my own personality I guess, a mixture of shyness and those North-east traits.

The jokes about hearing the sweetie wrappers rustling at Pittodrie are half-true. An Aberdeen audience, whether it's for football or performers on stage, is different to a Glasgow crowd. They tend to wait until they know what the outcome is before deciding whether to celebrate or show appreciation, whereas a Glasgow crowd's ready for a party from the first act to the last.

We were young parents soon after landing in Glasgow, with Amanda's arrival in 1969 and then her little sister Melanie in 1971, so it wasn't a time of partying and nights out every weekend – you were more likely to find us cruising down the Kilmarnock Road hoping the motion would send the girls off to sleep than out on the town. We lost a few dummies out of the window on those late-night trips! Our son Paul was born in 1978 to complete the family.

When we were out there was always a benefit to being a Rangers player. The best tickets, the best tables and the VIP treatment whether we were out for a meal or drinks. Because we had so many scattered in all parts of the east and west, it wasn't as though the whole squad socialised every week, but we did get together when we could.

The one night that sticks in my mind was going to the boxing and Sheila just about fainting because one of the fighters lost his tongue and it was bouncing off the canvas. That's what she thought – it was actually his gumshield! Between nights like that and supporters' club events it was fine to get together as a group and find out what made us all tick outside of football.

There's a certain privilege that goes with being on the playing staff at Ibrox. You get to meet a lot of good people who go out of their way to look out for you, welcome you into their family effectively. Whether you needed a new car or work done at the house, there was always someone who knew someone who would get you a good deal or make sure you were being treated the right way.

The flip side of that is that Glasgow wasn't all sweetness and light in the 1960s and 1970s. There have been enough true-crime documentaries over the years shining a light on that without me retelling the stories, but there was a mix of reality and urban myth around some of that. Inevitably we got to know and be around some of the characters who moved in those circles. I've always been a great believer that you choose your friends carefully, and that has stood me in good stead.

For every individual you learned to give a wide berth to, I met another thousand fantastic Rangers people, and even today that network is still in full force whether it has been a solicitor doing conveyancing work on a house purchase, a builder's merchant, or even the breeders we bought our two new puppies from.

Mind you, who knows? For every one of those helping hands there's maybe been another supporting the club from the other side of the city who has added a nought to a price tag or found an extra bit of work needing done!

I say that partly in jest, but when I was running a taxi business back in Aberdeen in later years there was one hackney inspector in particular who always seemed to relish when it was my turn for the regular vehicle checks. Let's say he could always find something when it was my car on the ramp, even if he had to look particularly hard. At least I was able to brighten up his day – it must have been dull otherwise.

Looking back, the eight years I spent at Ibrox were an incredible time and we packed an awful lot in to a relatively short period in our lives. We got married, welcomed two of our three children into the world, set up home in a new city and were met with open arms by the Rangers family.

Once you're part of that family you never leave it, and that's worth more to me than anything that was part of any contract.

THIRTEEN

'RATHER THAN SOAKING IN THE SUCCESS, WHAT FOLLOWED WAS UNCERTAINTY'

IT'S IMPOSSIBLE TO look back on Barcelona without addressing the scenes at the Nou Camp before, during and after the Dynamo Moscow game. It isn't something I have ever dwelled upon, and I don't intend to start doing so 50 years on, but I think it's important to provide a player's point of view.

Not being presented with the trophy on the pitch was a blow for us all. When you dream of winning a competition it's that moment shared with the supporters that's in your mind, not getting your first glimpse of the cup in the dressing room long after the final whistle.

The story of John Greig getting taken up to one of the many rooms deep inside the stadium for a hastily put together presentation is well told, but it wasn't just the chance to lift the trophy it was about the medal presentation and everything else we lost out on. I didn't win too many medals in my career, and it hurts that the most important of all wasn't presented properly on the night.

We had a presentation ceremony, led by the chairman, on the pitch at Ibrox ahead of the first game of the 1972/73 season that at least gave us the chance to enjoy the moment with the fans.

The medals had been engraved for us by the club for the occasion, and ever since that day it has sat side by side with the matching silver one from 1967. It's a pretty unique collection and is securely stored away from the house for safekeeping now with my other medals.

The reality is we didn't have any real inkling about the potential longer-term ramifications, particularly the European ban, on the night. From our perspective it was a case of over-exuberance from the supporters who ran onto the pitch to celebrate with the players they had followed through thick and thin.

When you consider the pain the Rangers support had gone through – shared by the players like myself who had been in the midst of it – on the domestic front, it was no surprise that the pent-up emotion spilled out in what was a huge travelling support.

Unfortunately, the Spanish authorities, and UEFA, hadn't anticipated it, and from my perspective it was a case of panic setting in among a police force that was pretty low in numbers in comparison to the crowd they were there to control.

Remember, there were no opposition fans – so there was no prospect of crowd trouble. It could have been handled so much better and there was no need for confrontation. Instead, it was a blunt-force approach and it escalated so quickly.

The warning signs were there from the off, with the excitement spilling from the stands onto the pitch in the minutes leading up to the game. We saw it again after the first goal, with the celebrations from the supporters who ran onto the park.

It was always going to happen again at key points in the game, and it didn't take a genius to predict it would be the same at the final whistle (or what the supporters thought was the final whistle, as it turned out).

The key thing for me was that after each of those moments,

the supporters had eventually made their way back to the stands once the initial rush had subsided.

We thought it would be the same at full time and when we left the pitch the expectation was that we would be back out once those initial celebrations had quietened down. And we very much viewed what was happening as celebrations rather than crowd trouble or riots as it was portrayed in some quarters.

They came on the pitch not knowing what they were doing or the longer-term repercussions it would have. Most, if not all, had been drinking through the day and into the night – not that it's an excuse, but I don't for a moment think they would have done the same if they'd been stone-cold sober. It was a case of the drink being in and the wit out.

I didn't hang about at full time to find out how it would pan out. It must have been the quickest I'd moved all night!

It wasn't a case of being scared because we knew it was only our fans on the pitch rather than anything that might escalate with opposition supporters, but there was the worry about getting caught up in the reaction from the Spanish police. I made my way through the crowd and straight down the tunnel, ready to catch a breath and celebrate. That euphoria which washes over you after a big win doesn't last for long, and you have to try to savour it while it's fresh.

I will always defend the genuine Rangers supporters. I knew many who were there and in later years I've met many more. They're good people and the criticism levelled by some was unfair.

The Rangers supporters were there to support their team and to savour what the events of the past 50 years tell us was a once-in-a-lifetime experience for so many.

When you speak to those who were there in the city and in the stadium on the night, the provocation and brutality from the local police are the factors that are cited again and again. The authorities who were supposed to be there to protect were the ones who acted as the aggressors against groups who had come to party.

I would never attempt to justify the actions of anyone overstepping the mark, but everything I've heard since and I saw at the time tells me that wasn't the case.

Whilst the Nou Camp was a great venue and has become more iconic as time has gone on, the organisation of the final wasn't perfect. Policing and stewarding were a major part of that, and it was down to the Spanish hosts and UEFA to get it right.

In contrast, the Nuremberg final in 1967 felt like a far better organised and a far bigger occasion in my view. The aftermath of '72 served to reinforce that.

Rather than soaking in the success, what followed was uncertainty about what punishment the club would face.

There was a potential European Super Cup showdown against European Cup winners Ajax that couldn't be firmed up until it was clear whether we would be allowed by UEFA to play any form of European games.

Eventually we did play Ajax, as part of the centenary celebrations in 1973. It was a privilege to be part of the 100-year anniversary and all that revolved around those games.

If you look in the record books you'll see the first teams to contest the European Super Cup were Ajax and AC Milan in 1974. That was the first official UEFA-sanctioned competition, with the Italians beaten 6-1 over two legs, but it was actually ourselves and Ajax who can lay claim to taking part in the inaugural challenge.

The Dutch were dominating European football – Ajax had won the European Cup for three consecutive years and had followed Feyenoord – and were determined to underline their credentials as the best of the best.

It was a journalist at the *De Telegraaf* newspaper in the Netherlands who came up with the idea of a showdown between the European Cup winners and the holders of the European Cup Winners' Cup on the back of the 1972 season, and it came to fruition in January 1973. The Ajax hierarchy were keen, UEFA less so given they'd just hammered us with a ban on the back of Barcelona.

The Dutch have never been too keen on being told what to do, so went ahead with their plans and made arrangements for the double-header.

It was about glory for a fantastic Ajax side, who liked the taste of picking up silverware in Europe, but there was also a commercial side to it. The newspaper had bankrolled it, with the intention of creating revenue streams for them as well as the two clubs involved. It also tied in nicely with the centenary, a good showpiece for those celebrations, and everyone was a winner, off the field at least!

Ajax were a very good side, with Johan Cruyff in all his pomp. They played the game the right way and there's absolutely no shame in saying they deserved to win over those two games. By no means were we outclassed, and on another day it might have been different. We were playing one of the best club sides in the world and considered ourselves a match for them in every department.

The huge difference in that era was that a club like Ajax could keep hold of its superstars for a longer period than they can now, just as Rangers could. There wasn't the same financial gulf between leagues. Although English and Italian clubs were a cut above in terms of the rewards they could offer, it wasn't impossible for sides outside of those countries to retain talent.

As a consequence, there wasn't the same turnover in squads and not the same movement between European countries. If I look back over my eight seasons at Ibrox, I reckon I could list every signing we made without blinking. Alex Ferguson, Orjan Persson, Colin Stein, Alex MacDonald, Peter McCloy, Tommy

McLean were among them, but there was really just one a year over that period. That was supplemented by the youngsters brought through, with the aim of improving the team with quality year on year rather than going for quantity.

It was all geared towards building a squad that could compete regularly for honours at home and abroad, but those European ambitions had to be put on hold in the wake of Barcelona as we awaited a cut-and-dried decision on what the governing body would do.

The deliberation on our punishment rumbled on for months. The initial two-year European ban was appealed by the club and the SFA and it went to a UEFA hearing in Zurich. To nobody's real surprise the original decision was upheld. It was the players who paid the biggest price, deprived of the chance to play at the highest level.

As a squad we couldn't have done anything differently and I'm not sure there was much the club could have done either. Before kick-off the manager had even tried to remonstrate with some of the rowdier sections of the crowd, above and beyond the call of duty I would say.

The club introduced stewards, Willie Waddell made speeches underlining the commitment to upholding standards. Not in a million years could you accuse Rangers of not responding appropriately. I don't think anything would have made a difference – the outcome seemed to have been decided, probably before we set off from the airport in Barcelona.

I come back to the point that all of those measures were targeted at a minority who attach themselves to the club, not the genuine Rangers support as I know it. A support that's about passion, loyalty and, above all else, good humour.

What I've never been able to relate to is the hatred that can envelop the game. I've heard and seen it on all sides, although I can honestly say in all my years living in Glasgow and those as a frequent visitor I've never once been abused by a Celtic supporter.

My relationship with Celtic players was no different to that with those from any other team – there were some gentlemen and friends, and others who I wouldn't describe as either and would cross the road to avoid.

I got on well with Billy McNeill, Jim Craig and Tommy Gemmell, to name just three who represented the club with distinction in the way they performed on the pitch and the way they conducted themselves off of it. There was a mutual respect in that we understood what it meant to play in that environment.

The Celtic supporters were generally respectful towards me – I hope a sign that they appreciated I played the game in the right spirit. The way I played could be seen as showboating, but even in Old Firm games it was never done with the intention of riling the opposition or fans. Well, maybe just a little bit.

Likewise, I never saw Rangers supporters have anything other than good-natured banter with the Celtic players of our era.

I'm not blinkered to the problems associated with football in Glasgow. There is a misconception that somehow the actions of a minority went unchallenged until recently, but that isn't the case. There was a game when Willie Waddell took to the touchline with a loudhailer to encourage supporters to channel their energy in the right way.

I far prefer to focus on the positives and the passion there is in the city for football, and I've seen that as a player and a spectator.

For my son's first Old Firm game we were standing in the East Enclosure; it was the 1990s, not too long before the terracing disappeared for good to be replaced by seats. That's a bit of a rite of passage, the intensity and energy that standing created has been really difficult to replicate.

As much as being in the thick of it can feel intimidating, particularly for an Old Firm game, it is generally full of humour.

Football has always been a working-class sport, where people come to vent for 90 minutes and release the pressures of the week. I understand that, even if it's alien to me in so many ways – Aberdonians aren't renowned for starting the singing.

What we aren't immune to, though, is the tribalism that's both good and bad in football. The rivalry between my two old clubs over the past few decades has gone well beyond the point of good nature.

I was born an Aberdonian, three of my grandchildren were too. The city was home for large swathes of my life and will always be part of me.

I'm proud to have played for Aberdeen Football Club and still appreciate when the former players' club magazine drops through the letterbox. As a club the Dons are an example to many others in terms of the way they treat their former players and work hard to make sure you feel part of that group. It is done the right way.

I played more than 100 games in a red shirt – blood, sweat and tears.

From the perspective of the supporters, however, I did commit the cardinal sin of swapping red for blue. Believe it or not, more than half a century on it's still a problem for a minority, albeit a decreasing number given the passage of time! I've got broad shoulders and have always brushed it off, but as you get older you think back and wonder why anyone would think they can act that way.

It happens on all sides – Hibs v. Hearts, United v. Dundee, Rangers v. Celtic. It's just a shame people can't leave the rivalry at the stadium gates and treat each other with respect.

I think British football supporters in general are more aware than ever of their responsibilities to represent their club in the right way. That message has to keep being reinforced, and I think the clubs have stepped up in that regard.

The issues we have seen in European competition, both at international level with the abuse England players have received, and club level with ties against some European teams in recent years, show there is a long way to go before the game gets where it needs to be. It doesn't mean anyone should stop trying; everyone can do their bit.

FOURTEEN

'ONE OF THE FEW MAJOR REGRETS I HAVE IN FOOTBALL'

THE AFTERMATH OF any big game, even the biggest of them all, is always a strange one. The day after the night before, it's back down to earth with a bump. One day we were together and celebrating and the next it was the start of the summer holidays.

It wasn't unusual for groups to head back to Ibrox over the close season to keep ticking over, and the summer of 1972 was no different. But the parade at the ground was really the last occasion we were together as a team. By the time we came back for pre-season, there were already moves afoot for some, and the prospect of others looking for a fresh challenge.

On top of that, we had a new manager in Jock Wallace.

It wasn't a huge surprise to us as players. It always felt like Jock was being groomed for the big job, and he attacked his coaching role with the confidence of a man with ambitions to keep progressing. He was a powerful character, in a different way to Willie Waddell and his quieter authority.

What we hadn't really expected was the timing. To take a step back after one of the most important wins in the club's history was bold, but Waddell had a wily side to him. The opportunity to move upstairs was perfectly timed for him in many ways. It meant he could still have a major influence without the day-to-day involvement in running the team. It also preserved his legendary status for evermore, unblemished by anything that might follow.

As it happened, the squad he'd assembled went on to sweep the boards domestically – so the personal gamble maybe didn't pay off. If he had held off he would perhaps have had some more silverware to his credit. History would suggest Wallace's more energetic style was the catalyst for that success and it was the right time to strike out on his own.

To give credit where it's due, the introduction of the General Manager's post made perfect sense. A club like Rangers needs layers of leadership, and when he had arrived that didn't exist. The manager was exactly that. Not just responsible for the team, but for just about every aspect from commercial operations through to logistics.

He proved to be adept at all of that, but juggling it with shaping a team and squad was a major ask.

In the run to Barcelona, it was Waddell himself who had scouted the opposition, racking up the air miles criss-crossing from France to Portugal, from Italy to Germany and onwards to Russia.

Redeveloping the ground was another of his very personal quests following the disaster – a full-time job in itself and one that he was emotionally invested in. There was no better man to lead in that period. He did it with dignity, authority and compassion.

It made sense to split the roles, although it didn't make the announcement any less seismic from a Scottish football perspective.

Wallace's appointment wasn't universally accepted at the time, at least not outside of the club. The media saw it as either brave or foolish. He was, in managerial terms, a young man being challenged to take on what was the biggest job in British club football without a track record to point to.

He was clearly trusted by Waddell. He had taken Jock to Ibrox from Hearts and set him on the path that led to the manager's office. They had been a good partnership, with different strengths and weaknesses, but on the back of Barcelona it felt as though there was a mood for change and to step up the pace of the modernisation.

He had spent time out at coaching schools in Germany and was part of the new breed of tracksuit managers, a big change from Scot Symon in his bowler hat! Jock was promising attacking football and more goals, although I don't think there was a major shift. We always had players who posed a threat and liked to get the ball down and play.

Waddell still had a major say on everything, and my instinct, particularly in those early days, would be that included on the football side.

It was telling that Waddell kept the manager's office. Jock found himself in a smaller room under the stand, like an attic space with a sloping roof. You would ask him something, big or small, and he wouldn't give you an answer straight away – I'm guessing he went to check with Waddell first. That would have changed with time I'm sure, but it felt like an uncomfortable set-up.

In hindsight, the reshuffle behind the scenes marked the beginning of the end for me, but that wasn't the way I was looking at things initially in that summer of 1972.

I was on the back of my best-ever season, with a European medal in my pocket. My only thoughts were about more success with Rangers and about the potential to get back into the thoughts of the Scotland manager Tommy Docherty.

By that stage I hadn't been capped for five years, but two broken legs in-between had been a factor. With that behind me, there was a lot to aim for. The World Cup in 1974 should have been a realistic target.

By the time the finals in Germany came around, I was heading towards a very different destination. Arbroath, to be precise.

I've been asked many times over the years if I feel I should have had more than the two caps I won for Scotland. The honest answer is yes, but it isn't something I dwelled on at the time or have done since.

To play for your country is something every schoolboy dreams of, and I got the chance to do that, so it would be wrong to complain.

It was obviously an honour to play for Scotland, but in that brief experience I found it could be a bit cliquey when the squads got together. You had the Rangers players together, the Celtic contingent and the England-based players who tended to gravitate towards each other.

It always sticks in my mind: playing in the Scottish league select, while I was still with Aberdeen, and coming off thinking I'd spent 90 minutes as piggy in the middle. The Rangers players passed to each other, and the Celtic players did the same!

My biggest regret isn't about my own international career but that my brother Doug wasn't honoured. I know I'm not alone in saying he is the best uncapped defender Scotland has ever produced, and it staggers me that, with all the quality he had, Doug didn't get the call. He did of course represent the SFA in the boardroom as a respected committee member, during his time as a Dundee United director, and carried himself with the same grace as he did on the pitch.

In terms of my own international career, it promised much but ultimately didn't take off in the way I or others might have expected.

My debut was while I was still with Aberdeen, picked for a match against the Netherlands just before I made the move to

Rangers. It was May 1966 against the Dutch at Hampden and not the type of match dreams are made of – we lost 3-0 and didn't do ourselves justice.

It was the first time in ages that it was an all Scottish-based team that was named, given there was such a strong Anglo contingent usually.

I think the supporters, and possibly the players, thought we just had to turn up to win because the Dutch were going through a difficult spell. We got hammered – the goals were flying in from 40 yards and all sorts.

On the plus side, it turned out to be a good introduction to my future teammates. John Greig was captain, Ronnie McKinnon was in the heart of the defence, Davie Provan on the left with Willie Johnston and Willie Henderson on the wings. It gives an indication of the strength of the Rangers squad at that time.

Andy Penman, another future Ibrox teammate, was brought in while starring for Dundee. Pat Stanton and Jim Scott, both at Hibs, were also called for the first time after we had all played for a Scotland select against Leicester City in a testimonial for Alex Dowdells.

I was only 22 at that time, just a boy really. Given I went on to play more than 300 games for Rangers after that, captained the team, played and won in Europe and went on to be player of the year in Scotland, it would have been fair to assume it would be the start of a long international career.

Instead, there was just one more appearance to follow. That came two years later in Amsterdam, this time a 0-0 draw with the Dutch in the Olympic Stadium.

John, Ronnie and Willie Henderson were still in the side but there was more of an Anglo feel to it. Charlie Cooke, by then starring in England, was there along with his Chelsea sidekick Eddie McCreadie and Bobby Moncur of Newcastle United.

Rangers were on tour in Scandinavia at that point, so our group flew down from Copenhagen to meet up with the squad.

That included George McLean and I always remember big Dandy, who probably missed as many as he scored in his career but had that brilliant knack of being in the right place to get on the end of things, saying to the manager when we were sitting down to breakfast the next day: 'Right boss, when's the next game?' That was big George – he'd had one of those nights where nothing went in, but he was still full of confidence and never let it get to him.

And that, at the age of 25, was that.

In fact, I didn't even get the caps when I played. Back then a physical cap wasn't awarded for every game, so it wasn't until the early 2000s, after the SFA set about retrospectively awarding caps, that I received mine. It was a nice gesture and appreciated by all of the players who received them.

I played my best football long after that second and last appearance, but for whatever reason my face didn't fit. Maybe I was seen as a luxury player, maybe it was just a series of unfortunate coincidences – the wrong player in the wrong position in the wrong era. There was, in hindsight, an embarrassment of riches for Scotland at that time – north and south of the border we were blessed with some fantastic talent. There were a lot of special players.

Would I put myself in that category? Absolutely! But you can't get too hung-up on the decisions you can't have any influence on.

It galls me now to see players retiring from international football. The only person who should make that call is the manager. I would never have said no to Scotland, and I can't relate to those who do at all. If you're picked, then you're fit enough and good enough to be involved.

In saying that, I did make one call in those early days that did dent my cap tally – declining the invitation to tour the world with Scotland in the summer of 1967. It was a seven-country marathon across the globe with a month of fixtures taking in Israel, Iran, Malaysia, Hong Kong, Australia, New Zealand and Canada.

That would have boosted the appearance total in one swoop, but I had another big match pencilled in. Sheila and I were due to be married on 10 June, five days before the end of the tour, and we couldn't get it rearranged at short notice. We'd originally settled on 17 June, which would have fallen after that trip, but it had been moved forward because we couldn't get a hotel to host the reception and there was just no way around it.

It wasn't the easiest conversation to have with Bobby Brown, the Scotland manager at the time. Bobby was a lovely man and in later years we attended many functions together, supporting the Erskine Foundation in particular in our role as proud patrons of the charity, and as ever he was full of understanding that day. Bobby is sadly missed and I was proud to serve alongside him as a patron of the charity, a role I continue to hold. Special mention must go to Ian Nicol, who has run successful fundraising events in Aberdeen for the foundation for many years.

It was after a game against Airdrie at Broomfield that Bobby asked me to join the squad. I'd scored a penalty that day to put us top of the league and my stock was high. He'd spoken to Scot Symon before approaching me, and I doubt he had many rejections – but Bobby understood the predicament. It wasn't even a decision in all honesty; I was never going to let football get in the way of the wedding.

The ceremony went ahead as planned at the Kirk of St Nicholas in the heart of Aberdeen. It was big news at the time, there were lots of newspaper reporters and photographers in attendance, and a few hundred well-wishers gathered outside under glorious blue skies. Lewis Thom, who I'd come through alongside at Aberdeen, was my best man, and John Greig, Alex Smith, Davie Provan and Alex Willoughby made the trip up to fly the Rangers flag.

While 2022 represents the 50th anniversary of Barcelona, it also brings our 55th wedding anniversary. That's far more important to me than anything that happened on a football pitch.

Sheila is the most courageous person I know. Beautiful, intelligent, with a wicked sense of humour – but above all else so incredibly incredibly strong. Life has not been easy and I'm sorry I haven't always made it that way. Through it all she has been the one who has been there for us all.

Our wedding day was the proudest of my life, and the end of the reception at The Treetops Hotel was the start of a new chapter for us, a farewell to the city.

Sheila, who had moved to Aberdeen from Oxfordshire with her family in her schooldays, and I had been together for a few years, and at the time I was commuting to Glasgow from the North-east. It was long before the dual carriageway and a torturous journey, through every town and village along the route in my trusty little Mini.

After the wedding we honeymooned in France and then came back to set up home in Glasgow. I think we both would have been content if that move west had been for life. Football doesn't work that way.

Barcelona in '72 proved to be the peak; the paths were leading away from Ibrox. Within two years I'd gone from the highest of highs to facing up to the fact the Rangers chapter was closing.

When I left in November 1974 I was turning 31 years old and had lost months kicking my heels in the reserves. My last first-team game was in February that year in a 3-2 defeat against Arbroath in the league.

I always had it my mind that football was a short career. At Aberdeen, I'd watched the captain Jimmy Hogg leave at 28 to go into the Highland League because professional clubs considered anyone nearing 30 as finished. Now you can get a four-year contract at 30 – although I appreciate players are fitter. A lot of that is to do with the conditioning work and sports science, but there's also something around improvements in society. Most families are better off and better fed, so there's a better base to build athletes from. I say most, all too aware that isn't the same for all unfortunately.

The creation of physically strong, fast and fit players is an area where the academy system can be applauded. From a young age, kids are better educated about nutrition and are also working on strength and conditioning as teenagers in a way which we wouldn't even have dreamt of. That's the only concession I'll make as far as the success of youth coaching is concerned. I'll come back to that.

In the end it wasn't fitness or age that led me to leave, it was about personalities and two strong-willed individuals.

There's a misconception that Jock Wallace and I didn't get on – that couldn't be further from the truth. We were very different characters but there was a mutual respect and I enjoyed training under him. Hard work has never scared me, and I shared his determination to win. We were far more similar in that respect than most would imagine.

Aside from that, although he played on his reputation as the hard taskmaster, there was actually more ball work in his sessions than I'd been used to under most other coaches. Eddie Turnbull at Aberdeen would have been the other who had a similar approach.

We got on well on a personal level too; we travelled in to training together from Newton Mearns pretty regularly. All of that doesn't point to a rift.

As someone with Rangers in my heart, I celebrated what he went on to achieve in his first spell as manager, and what so many of those I'd been privileged to share a dressing room with delivered under him.

That doesn't mean we didn't have our differences, both during and after my time at Rangers, and I don't think it's impossible for a relationship like that to play out in football.

So once and for all, let's break it down.

There's a theory that I just was never in Jock's plans. The facts don't really ring true as far as that's concerned – in his first season in charge he picked me for 43 of 51 competitive games, not the actions of a manager who didn't value or trust a player.

In his first competitive game in charge, a 2-0 win against Clydebank on the day we paraded the European Cup Winners' Cup to a packed Ibrox, I was there at No. 6 and in the heart of the defence.

What did mark the beginning of the end for me at Ibrox wasn't the arrival of Wallace in the manager's chair but of Tom Forsyth in the dressing room, even if that wasn't the intention. Tom was Jock's first major signing and was brought in as a midfielder, but it wasn't working out for him in there. He was better suited as a stopper.

The manager and I had conversations about me swapping roles and moving back into the midfield, where I did play quite a few games that season. At that stage in my career, on the back of my best-ever season and as Scotland's player of the year at sweeper, it seemed a strange logic to me, but I would have played anywhere on the park for Rangers and I told him that – as long as I was playing it didn't matter where he wanted to put me.

The issue that I had was the way Jock wanted me to play that position. He wasn't looking for creativity and culture, he wanted me, with my 30s looming, to become a tiger-tackling ball winner in the middle of the park. For anyone who saw me play, that wasn't me. I've no doubt Jock appreciated my qualities, but he wanted more, and he wanted something I couldn't give him – or, more to the point, something I just fundamentally disagreed with.

In any workplace, if you don't agree with what you're being asked to do you've got two choices: you either put your principles to one side or you clear your desk. I've never been one to back down, so for me there was only one choice. I told Jock that if that was the way he wanted me to play then he would be better to pick someone else.

I never had a major fall-out with him, but in the way we wanted to play the game we were poles apart.

Sure enough, he dropped me for the next game. I'll always remember sitting in the boot-room after that match at Ibrox, away from the rest of the boys who had played, and Jock coming in. They'd lost 3-1 to Dundee and he wasn't in the best of spirits. He thought I was smiling, I'd argue otherwise. Either way, Jock swung a punch, I dodged it and told him he'd have to be quicker than that.

That's a glimpse of how things could be. I never held it against him, and we weren't on bad terms afterwards.

We were two strong characters, and as manager he held the power, so I had no expectation that there would be any other outcome than me moving on. I never asked to leave, but I did tell him not to pick me unless he wanted me to play the game my way. It was one of those situations that crop up every season in football, and I was big enough to look after myself.

Even before it all came to a head the writing was on the wall.

I was left out of the Scottish Cup final team by Jock in 1973, a pretty big blow given I'd played in every single tie up to that game. Who scored the winner? Tom Forsyth. It's a funny old game, as they say. I did get a medal by virtue of my appearances and being the substitute on the day, but I've never once looked at it.

It's difficult to feel part of it when you're on the touchline, but I am proud to have played my part in helping the boys reach the final.

Missing that game hurt. I'd put in the hard yards all season long, and to be sidelined for the showpiece was a big blow. Purely tactical or maybe a case of being shown who was boss? Only Jock could have told you that.

Any player who tells you they take that kind of decision in their stride is, I would say, either lying or in the wrong sport. You want to play every game, especially the big ones, but it's the manager's choice – I've been in that seat myself and there are difficult calls to make.

Jock came in before the game and told me I wasn't starting but made a big play of the fact he was naming me as a substitute. Maybe I should have been grateful? I think all I replied was 'big deal' and never uttered another word about it.

I wouldn't speak ill of anyone who is no longer with us or of someone who gave the club very distinguished service, with Jock and Tom both in that category.

For me it was a case of the right place at the wrong time, and when that happens it's about dusting yourself down and looking forward, not back.

Do I wish I had been part of the team for the title win in 1975? Of course, but not if it meant not being true to myself. Letting my heart rule my head has always been a blessing and a curse.

Jock had tremendous success and won the league to stop ten in a row. I'm the first to admit that by playing the way I saw the game it might never have happened. He found a way to win.

What happened next is one of the few major regrets I have about the choices I made in football. I could have gone back to Aberdeen, there were discussions about a swap deal involving their player Ian Purdie, but that fell through.

There were a few other options open to me.

I should never have left – I should have worked harder to find a solution to stay. I would have loved to have seen my days out in a Rangers shirt.

I could have picked up the phone to Eddie Turnbull, who I'm certain would have taken me to Hibs. Eddie had tried to take me back to Aberdeen in the late 1960s before he went to

Easter Road, just as Davie White's tenure at Ibrox came to an end. Davie was sacked the day after those talks had started and the deal was off – the rest, as they say, is history. If that had gone through, I would have missed out on Barcelona and all that means to me.

Instead of any of those potential choices I made the decision to join Arbroath. Difficult to imagine this season's player of the year ending up at Gayfield, but that's exactly what happened.

To provide a bit of context, they were in the top division when I moved, and it was a player-coach role, so an opportunity to cut my teeth and prepare for management.

Arbroath were being pretty shrewd in the transfer market, bringing in experience and players who had maybe fallen out of favour at the bigger clubs but still had something to offer. Jimmy Bone and Gordon Marshall had come in from Celtic, Andy Penman and me from Rangers.

Albert Henderson the manager was someone I knew and respected. Albert's brother Bobby had been best friends with my big brother Jim, so again there was an element of heart ruling head when the approach came. I'd known Albert since I was a kid. He was an Aberdeen Lads' Club boy too, and there was an emotional pull.

They also offered me an incredibly good deal, but that wasn't my motivation. I wanted to play.

It was a culture shock going from the luxury of Ibrox and that cosseted existence to being a part-time player at Gayfield. By that stage, we were living in Dunblane, and I was travelling east twice a week for training, my first experience of that semi-pro set-up.

I joined in November of 1974, and it turned out to be a short stay. Within a few months the committee who ran the club came to me and sounded me out about taking over as manager. Maybe I was being naïve, but my response was to ask what Albert thought of that idea. He had no idea – and they had no idea that my loyalties were with him, not them.

I didn't have the heart to tell him what was going on behind his back. I think it would have done more harm than good. He was the longest serving manager in Scotland, and I didn't want to do anything to rock the boat for him.

Instead, I told him it wasn't working for me and I wanted to move on. Like the gent he was, he gave it some thought and eventually agreed.

Albert went on to spend another five years in charge at Gayfield – 18 years in total. It was a remarkable length of time to lead one club, and he did it in the right manner.

Arbroath had been promoted from the old Second Division to the top league in the summer of 1972. They'd finished level on points with Dumbarton, losing out on the title on goal difference, and getting up to the higher level gave the club a bit of impetus to build on.

Albert quite rightly got a lot of credit for keeping them in the league at the first attempt and consolidating the following year. I saw it described as using home-grown talent and 'whatever leftovers he can pick up from richer kitchens', and that was one way of looking at it, even if I'm not sure I appreciate being thrown into the category of a leftover!

When you saw bigger clubs – the likes of Kilmarnock, Airdrie, Falkirk, Dunfermline and Clyde – dropping down into the Second Division it was always going to be a struggle for Arbroath to keep their head above water, but they were prepared to invest. They paid £10,000 to take me to Angus, not an insignificant fee for them.

It turned out to be folly really – with the top flight being culled from 18 teams to ten at the end of the season to form the Premier Division. That had been voted upon in the summer of 1974, so everyone knew what was around the corner. To finish in the top ten and earn a place in that bold new era was practically impossible for Arbroath, but they were obviously determined to give it a good go.

There had been conversations about league reconstruction going back to my early days at Aberdeen. All sorts of approaches had been considered to try and bring a spark back to the domestic game and increase crowds.

The bigger league brought more variety, but not necessarily the competitive edge that you need. By the tail end of the season, you ended up with a glut of teams in the middle of the table who were playing a lot of meaningless fixtures, so you could see the attraction in shrinking it down and making as many matches as possible count.

The issue with that is you do it at the expense of the clubs like Arbroath – for them, just being in that top division was success and it meant their supporters were able to see the likes of Rangers, Celtic, Aberdeen, Hearts and Hibs at Gayfield.

It was those clubs that lost out through reconstruction, and I don't think it's fair to say they didn't bring anything to the party. There were still the occasional upsets and, speaking with my Rangers hat on rather than from an Arbroath perspective, there were plenty of tricky afternoons for the big clubs when they had to visit some of the less glamorous locations on the Scottish footballing map. The likes of Cowdenbeath and Stirling Albion had stints mixing with the big boys, and it's difficult to imagine those days ever returning under the current set-up. For those teams it was about staying up if at all possible, grabbing points wherever they could.

By the time I arrived at Arbroath in the winter of 1974, the perennial struggle to stay off the foot of the table was well and truly underway. Hearts, who had a horrific start to the season, and for a spell Partick Thistle, looked as though they might spare the blushes from an Arbroath perspective, but over the course of a season those two pulled themselves away from danger. I'd moved on by the time their fate was sealed, with Arbroath finishing rock bottom.

One of the strange experiences of that short spell at Arbroath was going back to Ibrox as a visiting player. For eight years I'd been going in the front door as a Rangers man and this time was pitching up and having to go in the away dressing room.

Rangers and Celtic were neck and neck at the top of the league, and a defeat would have been disastrous. None of that matters once you're in another team's colours, and we were desperate for points for our own reasons. As it happened, the form book didn't lie, and it was the home side which ran out 3-0 winners against a side featuring two veterans of the run to Barcelona in myself and Andy Penman.

Given the personal connection, I would have loved nothing more than managing to help Albert turn things around, but it wasn't to be. That was the last season they ever played at the top level and that's not a piece of history any player wants to lay claim to being part of.

FIFTEEN

'THERE WAS NO SHORTAGE OF STARDUST AROUND THE LA AZTECS'

AFTER ARBROATH AND the frustration of leaving Ibrox, it felt like the right time for a radical change of direction.

Kai Johansen, who had been such a popular figure during his playing days at Ibrox, had moved to South Africa to play in the early 1970s and by then was manager of the Arcadia Shepherds.

I'd always got on well with Kai – I can't think of anyone who wouldn't, he was such a fantastic character. We used to travel in to work together. I was out in Newton Mearns and would pick him up at Pollockshields, and I kept in touch when he moved overseas. When things came to an end at Arbroath we spoke about the opportunities out there, and it went from there pretty quickly.

The Shepherds, based in Pretoria, were a big name in South Africa, and Kai had success with them, winning the treble the season before I landed. That had won him plenty of friends and probably loosened the purse strings too, so he had leeway in the transfer market.

On balance, it seemed like too good a chance to turn down and it was an opportunity to try something different after playing the same teams and at the same grounds in Scotland for a decade and a half. This was a chance to have the sun on our backs, a pool in the garden and something completely new.

I told Arbroath they could tear up the contract, and we packed our bags for South Africa.

It was part-time football in South Africa, albeit well rewarded, so I went back to the profession I'd started in as a teenager in Aberdeen in structural steel engineering. I loved the job, working on big projects including the tender for the Durban railway station redevelopment, but wasn't as enamoured with the football.

The quality wasn't great, even with the influx of Brits. The Arcadia Shepherds, given the success they had, were able to pull in big names – we had Bobby Charlton for a guest spell, with a lot of the English players coming out for short periods to top up the bank balance and soak up the sun. George Best had a stint with Jewish Guild in Johannesburg at around the same time as I was out there. Jack Charlton and Kevin Keegan also had stints in South Africa at different stages.

While on the pitch it was a struggle, the biggest issue was, of course, an obvious one – apartheid.

I say it was obvious, but I have to hold my hands up and say I was naïve about what I was heading into. From afar you knew it was a troubled country and that segregation was still part of life, but I had no real concept of the extent of apartheid until I saw it at first hand.

The National Football League that we were playing in, to give just one example, was only for white players despite the incredible passion the black players and supporters had for the game. A whole generation of black players were prevented from playing at the top level, confined to separate divisions which didn't have the profile or the standing of the main competition.

The year after my time in South Africa, the country's football association was formally expelled by FIFA. Football was one of the final sports to take a stand, not for the first or last time.

It meant the national team and club teams couldn't compete over their own borders and likewise visits from sides from outside weren't sanctioned.

Individual players from overseas were still free to ply their trade, and many Brits did continue to travel out. By then, I'd already made up my mind and moved on. In 1977 there was reform in South African football with the merging of the segregated leagues, but even then there was a limit on the number of black players permitted in each side. It sounds like a different world, but that was the reality.

It was common for white families to have black housekeepers. We had no intention of following suit, but relented after speaking to a lady, Francine, who had called at our door hoping to find work. When Francine would eat with us, she wouldn't feel comfortable being at the table – she would physically turn away, as if she shouldn't be there with us. It was heart-breaking to see the way she had been worn down, made to feel that way over a lifetime. Over time she grew to feel more comfortable and knew her family were an extension of our own and always welcome.

Unfortunately, we were the exception. When Francine's daughters were in the garden playing with Melanie and Amanda, neighbours stoned the four girls just for being together. When you saw how that hatred started at such a young age, it was no surprise grown women like Francine were made to feel like second-class citizens. I hope we did what little we could to show her and her husband and children that it didn't have to be that way, that it shouldn't be that way.

While we tried to comprehend what we were surrounded by in day-to-day life, work and football carried on.

I picked up a runners-up medal in the National Football League Cup when we narrowly lost out to Highlands Park at the Rand Stadium in Johannesburg. That Castle Cup, as it was better known, was a huge game in the country, supporters lining the streets outside the stadium and more than 30,000 packed inside. We lost that game 2-0 and finished fifth in the league, with Highlands Park winning both competitions.

Nothing that happened on the park could offset the problems in South Africa at that time, and we knew from very early on that we wouldn't settle there.

There was another more appealing challenge waiting around the corner, and once again there was a Scottish connection to thank.

It was the Seattle Sounders who took me to America from South Africa in 1976, with Jimmy Gabriel getting in touch while I was in Pretoria to invite me to the States.

Jimmy, who I'd played against when he was at Dundee and alongside in the Scotland under-23 side, had joined as player-assistant manager with what was a new team and looking for temporary reinforcements.

Jimmy, who passed away in the States in 2021, built his life in America long after the rest of us moved back home and he made a huge impact in Seattle and the surrounding region at just about every level of football there.

There were quotas for overseas players in the league, and he had a batch lined up to join Harry Redknapp and Geoff Hurst on his roster. John 'Tiger' McLaughlin was another of Jimmy's Scottish recruits, although it was their time together at Everton that was the main link, as well as Gordon Wallace of Dundee. Beyond my time, Bobby Moore was another to wear the Sounders colours under Jimmy.

In the meantime, there was a spot for me to slot into. We trained near the Boeing aerospace factory but played downtown at the new Kingdome, opened earlier that year. It had a capacity of nearly 60,000 at that time and was a big cavernous indoor arena, perfect for shielding from the harsh winters of Washington state.

Billy Graham's evangelical show was actually the biggest draw in its first year – bringing in more spectators than the Eagles or Evel Knievel. There are very few stadiums I've graced that can boast that type of line-up in the space of a few months!

Rather than uproot for the sake of a month's contract, I moved out to Seattle on my own, and Sheila and the girls went back home to Aberdeen. I spent a fair bit of time with Jimmy and his family, and we'd have a Tuesday night out with Harry and Geoff, but it was always going to be a short stint.

What it did was open the door for a permanent move to the LA Aztecs and, after the Scottish-type weather of Seattle, it was a pleasant contrast to pitch up in California. Sheila and the girls moved out to meet me there, and it was a fantastic lifestyle.

Again, there was an element of the old boys network at play, with quite a strong Scottish contingent right the way through the North American Soccer League.

It was Charlie Cooke, who was already out there with the Aztecs, who opened the door for me to join him.

There were plenty of quirks to playing in Los Angeles – not only did we have George Best on the playing roster, but there was an all-star cast associated with the club. From Alice Cooper and Rod Stewart to Elton John, who had become part of the ownership team – there was no shortage of stardust around the LA Aztecs, and it wasn't unusual to see famous faces on the training ground.

The club had been founded a couple of years previously when the North American Soccer League opened up bidding for an LA franchise. Jack Gregory, a football-loving doctor in the city with funds behind him, was successful, and the Aztecs were born. The story goes that he chose the name because he wanted a team to mirror the Aztec warriors – although the recruitment policy seemed to major on silk rather than steel.

By the time I arrived, the ownership had changed and Elton, or Sir Elton as I should probably address him, had been brought in by John Chaffetz, a lawyer who led the takeover, primarily to boost the profile and help build the crowds. I doubt he was ever in the office dealing with ticket stubs.

We averaged gates of around 8,000 and played out of El Camino College, with the club offices nearby at Redondo Beach.

We were managed by Terry Fisher, an up-and-coming American coach in his mid-20s who had been brought in from the University of Central Los Angeles. It was a big ask for someone so inexperienced to herd a group of seasoned players assembled from near and far, although in all honesty it was more a case of making sure we were in the right place at the right time.

There wasn't an awful lot of coaching done. We kept ourselves ticking over as best we could. To be fair, almost half a century on, Terry is still working in football, heading up youth football in Washington – so he has gone the distance.

I'd landed a bumper contract and the opportunity to be part of the rapid expansion of the league. On paper it was all good, and I enjoyed the experience, but as was the case for so many who went out to follow the same path it was never going to be a long-term move.

For all the league benefited from the introduction of Best, Pelé and, in later years, Cruyff, the standards weren't as high as we had been used to. Those types of player were the exception – and I have to say what I saw of George, even in the twilight of his career, only reinforced what I knew about his special talent.

He was also in a good place personally at that stage, so drink wasn't a factor, and he was as fit as he had been in a long time I would guess. The Californian sunshine does no harm at all for ageing limbs, as we all had by then.

To my mind George was the best of his generation – over Pelé and Cruyff – and right up there with the best of all time. He could play anywhere – on the wing, as a full-back or even as a centre-half. He was a clever clever player.

The problem with the Aztecs was George didn't have too many players around him who were on the same wavelength. They'd pick the wrong pass and nine times out of ten that pass was trying to find George when it wasn't on – which ended up making him look bad. He could still turn it on, though, and he was top scorer in the season I was there. He scored some wonderful solo goals along the way and made the All Star team, the epitome of US soccer!

I had a huge amount of respect for him as a player and I can only speak about the character I saw, who was quite content and humble. The good times didn't last for George and, after I was back in Scotland, he slipped back into old ways after buying a bar in LA. It ended up with him being shipped out to Fort Lauderdale when the Aztecs lost patience.

I ended up playing against him while I was player-manager with Berwick Rangers during George's brief stint at Hibs. Davie Moyes (no, not that one), the enforcer in our team, started out trying to kick him off the park. I took Davie aside and told him to lay off – for one you don't kick George Best and for another by that stage his heart wasn't in it and the legs had gone too. We were better off with him on the pitch than them bringing on a substitute. It was sad to see, but like everyone he had a living to make. Every penny he earned came back through the gate in increased attendances, so I don't buy the argument that he somehow took advantage of Hibs.

The nature of the NASL meant a huge amount of travelling, even though we were split into regional conferences. Even games in the same state were a trek, but when you factored in cross-country flights it felt like you spent large chunks of your life on the road.

With the restriction on the number of overseas players that could be included in squads as they attempted to give it a more homegrown feel, there was a bit of rotation between the franchises.

When you look back at that roll call, it's impressive to see the number of top-quality players they managed to assemble. Unfortunately, it was a boom-and-bust approach, and without the buy-in of the paying public it was destined to fail.

The advent of the Major League Soccer in recent years – and the introduction of the likes of David Beckham, Steven Gerrard, Andrea Pirlo and Thierry Henry – had very familiar overtones, but there seems to be a far more sustainable business model behind it. Commercial nous has clearly developed over the years.

As much as it was fun while it lasted for me, the US was never home – it was another stop on the football journey and an experience to tick off the list.

SIXTEEN

'I REALISED AS MANAGER I WAS FREE TO PLAY THE WAY I LIKED'

IF THE INTEREST from Real Madrid in the 1960s was flattering, my next dalliance with one of the big names in European football falls into the category of the bizarre.

After all, how many players can say they turned down Paris Saint-Germain in favour of Berwick Rangers? I think it's safe to say I'm on my own.

From the timing to the location and the outcome, it was straight out of left field.

It was the autumn of 1976, and I was in the less than glamorous surroundings of the boardroom of the Berwick Salmon Fisheries Company, down at the harbour in the town, with the club's chairman Jim Reed.

I was still an LA Aztecs player, but I was there with their blessing to talk to Berwick about taking over as manager, and we were there to finalise the deal. Having been in South Africa and America for 18 months, it was the right time to come home.

I actually had another two years to run on my contract with the Aztecs but was home during the break in the American season and training with Alex Ferguson at St Mirren. He was keen to play me in a reserve game with a view to signing, but there were issues with international clearance as well as the Aztecs holding out for a fee. It was a no go.

Fergie was just starting out on his journey in coaching and was a man in a hurry, maybe with a point to prove. His big break at Rangers hadn't gone as planned and he wasn't ever going to let opportunities in management get away. He had that hunger right from the start. He dedicated himself to the profession and was single-minded in all that he did, from the first season in charge at East Stirlingshire onwards.

Although we only played together for a relatively short time, we struck up a good friendship at Ibrox. I was there when he got the news his time at the club was over, while we were on tour in Denmark. It was a tough day, followed by taking him for a big night out in Copenhagen to try and cheer him up.

As much as you remember the ones who were there for the good times, I think those who are there for you when the chips are down stick in the mind, and we did what all good friends would do at that time. Alex, even years later when he was in the full throes of life at Manchester United, would always return a call.

What I have never done is ask for favours in football and if I'd signed for him at St Mirren it would have been because we both knew I could do a job. Who knows where that would have led if we had been able to pair up at that stage, perhaps back to Aberdeen in some shape or form when he made that switch and everything that followed, but there's no sense in dwelling on what might have been.

I had a different path to follow, and it was taking me south. Berwick, through Jim, approached me about the job while I was over, and it opened my eyes to the chance to move into management earlier than I had expected. I went and spoke to them, and they had come to an arrangement with the owners in LA (who obviously didn't see dollar signs in the same was as they did when St Mirren were in for me), so it was a case of putting the finishing touches to the contract.

We were just about there and ready to complete everything when a phone call came through – it was Charlie Cooke. He was telling me not to sign anything.

Charlie, having spent so long in England with Chelsea, had contacts everywhere and he'd got wind of an opportunity for me with PSG. It was typical of him, ever the wheeler-dealer and with friends in all the right places.

To this day, I've no idea how Charlie tracked me down to that building, but the phone rang and Jim Reed, not knowing it could potentially scupper the deal he'd been working so hard to get over the line, passed me the receiver.

PSG were still a baby in football terms, founded in the late 1960s, but seemed to be going places under Velibor Vasovic, a Serb with a big reputation as a player and clearly big ambitions as a coach. I couldn't claim to know too much about French football – there wasn't the wall-to-wall TV coverage that we take for granted now and PSG certainly weren't a household name.

They were playing their football at the Parc des Princes and attracting decent crowds for a relatively new side, so it wasn't the worst proposition in the world. But then I'd done metalwork at school rather than languages, so Berwick was maybe a better bet!

I told Charlie I wasn't going away again to play in France, so it was a thanks but no thanks from me.

The real reason I politely declined, put the phone down and put pen to paper was that I'd already given my word and I'd been made so welcome. I've never once regretted that decision, and it's a nice story to tell the grandkids, who are more used to seeing Neymar and Mbappe rather than Smith on the back of PSG shirts.

It wasn't a lack of ambition, far from it. The chance to get my teeth into management had whetted my appetite, and I was desperate to get started. I didn't stop to think about what that really entailed or the scale of the task I was taking on.

Scottish football had been divided into three: Premier Division, First Division and Second Division.

Berwick were rooted in the bottom tier and when I came in were on a run of 25 games without a win, across two pretty miserable seasons. We went on to pick up 32 points from 26 games and steadied the ship in that first season.

Berwick were known for being run on a shoestring, although the club had pushed the boat out to bring me in. We were well looked after, with a house built right on the beach by the club for us at Spittal and club cars for Sheila and me. It's a great town, with the Geordie influence bringing the same type of warmth you find in Glasgow. We still have good friends there. We are still in touch with those we were closest to, including Margaret Johnson. Margaret and her husband George, who sadly passed away recently, were a great support and, together with their sons Chris and David, became good family friends.

Mind you, we were the only team in Scotland that needed a coach for home games. We would bus players down from Edinburgh to Shielfield and trained in the capital too. The scouting network extended into the north of England, with the players we brought in from the Newcastle area able to train with teams there and coming up the coast for games and regular sessions with the rest of the squad when it was practical to do that. It wasn't ideal, but we had to make compromises to get the right people into the club.

It quickly became clear the job at Berwick was huge. No matter if you have players with decent ability, when you are being beaten week in and week out the confidence just drains away. Even the best start to wonder if they're good enough to tie their own shoelaces.

Once I'd settled into the role we made pretty rapid progress, but it was a shock to the system in those first few months.

Overnight you go from playing to running the team and it takes a bit of adjustment. I remember playing in the first game at Berwick, and the trainer, Tom Davidson, shouted over about making a substitution. He was asking who I wanted to take off. I thought for a second and told him any of the other 10!

Being a full-time manager of a part-time team was a challenge. Two sessions a week isn't enough to get everything across that you want, but over time you can shape a team as you want it.

As a manager all I ever asked of players was that they did what they were good at and gave everything they had for the team. I wanted to help players grow and improve, but I hope I never tried to get anyone to do anything they weren't capable of.

There were a few strands to the Berwick job as I saw it: to build the belief back among those I would be keeping on, to recruit well to bolster a struggling squad and to bring some structure on and off the park.

I couldn't do that alone and I knew who I wanted beside me as assistant manager, Willie Mathieson. Willie and I had struck up a real bond while we were together at Ibrox. We were different players and characters, but there was a chemistry. Most importantly, I trusted him implicitly and knew we would work well together.

There was no ego with Willie, but he knew the game inside out and was a thinker. Where I was maybe a bit more off the cuff, he was an organiser and level-headed. It was a partnership that served Berwick well.

Tom, who had been at the club when I arrived, stayed on as part of the coaching team and we set about the rebuilding process.

I launched coaching sessions for youngsters in the area, hoping we could make inroads in an area that was dominated by rugby, as well as bringing in a reserve team to provide a pathway for the most promising young players from across the region.

That side must have had an average age of about 17, but I always thought bringing youngsters into that type of environment was the way to go. If you're 20 and haven't played full-blooded football there's little chance you'll make it – too many clubs, even at Premier League level, make the mistake of shielding youngsters for too long and it stunts development.

The first season was about stabilisation and then in 1977/78 we had a good tilt at the title, coming up just short. We finished five points off the top and missed out on promotion as Clyde and Raith Rovers went up.

We fell off the pace in the latter stages of the campaign as the squad was stretched to its limits, lacking the depth that was required to sustain a challenge.

Finance then was as big a hurdle as it is now for part-time teams. In that first season we posted a loss of £8,000 – big money when you consider that was almost 50 years ago. We were able to push admission prices up as the quality of the product improved, and gates continued to rise as results picked up – we broke the 1,000 average in that 1977/78 season, which was a significant achievement, and were one of the best-supported teams in the lower leagues.

Despite the distances involved, the travelling support grew and grew as results picked up too. By the time we eventually won the Second Division title in 1979, with a midweek game at Cowdenbeath, we had a pretty raucous group who were following us all over the country, and it made for a great atmosphere in that run to the title.

That 1978/79 campaign is the one that's still spoken about today in Berwick. We won the Second Division championship, but it was more than that. We did it in style and with smiles on our faces. To me that means everything.

What made it all the more satisfying is that we weren't out in front from the start – we had to come from pretty far back to win the league and we went on an incredible run towards the end of the season where we tore lots of good teams to shreds. We scored goals for fun and went out to attack every team we faced. I was confident in the group we had assembled at Shielfield and basically just let them go out and prove they were the best. Which they did.

I was 35 by then but was playing week in and week out – I was never going to drop myself! I was on set-pieces, penalties – you name it, I did it. I won the Second Division Player of the Year award that season and in more recent times was named the Berwick Rangers Player of the Millennium, so I think I was right to keep picking myself. I would say that!

What I realised was as manager I was free to play the way I liked. If I wanted to beat three men in the six-yard box and throw a few nutmegs, I could do that without answering to anyone.

I think, or at least I hope, by playing that way it gave the rest of the team the confidence to try things, and it was a pretty relaxed atmosphere. We still get back together every now and again, and what you realise looking back is that we had a special time together. Everyone has a story to tell and good memories, not just playing together but as friends.

You've got to enjoy playing.

We'd put together a good mix of players. Battlers like Davie Moyes, as I mentioned previously, and Stewart Wheatley, ball players like Jimmy Morton, willing runners like Gordon 'Pogo' Smith and livewires like Eric Tait and Peter Davidson. Eric and Peter in particular are Berwick legends and still revered by all who saw them play.

We had to be clever in the transfer market and look for rough diamonds we could polish. We were a selling club, that was the simple economic equation, and made some good gains. The sale of Peter Davidson to Queen's Park Rangers was one that balanced the books, just a couple of years after I'd brought him in from Newcastle Blue Star.

Tommy Docherty paid £40,000 for him on the back of the title win, although Peter loved it so much with us he was back on our books after a few months in London. He was a star for us and is one of the boys I'm still in touch with now.

Although I had to wheel and deal, I had decent backing as we began to build revenue through the gates and sponsorship. We spent a club record of £10,000 on Jimmy Morton when he came in from Brechin just in time for the start of the 1978/79 season. He scored a goal every second game from midfield, including his share of free-kicks, and we sold him to St Johnstone a year later for £30,000 so it was a good bit of business. Jimmy went on to be capped for the Scotland semi-professional team and was a talented boy, although the trips down from his home in Dundee to Berwick meant I didn't expect he'd be with us for too long.

Donnie McLean came in for £7,000 from Albion Rovers (big money at the time) and scored in his second game as we beat St Johnstone 2-0, putting them out of the League Cup over two legs. We brought in Calum Frame for a similar fee to go in as No. 1, and it felt like the team was coming together.

The best compliment I can pay that squad is to say there were an awful lot of players in the squad who shouldn't have been playing for Berwick – and that's not disrespecting a little club that I love. Pogo's a case in point – he came to us after being released by Hearts, and Billy McNeill was close to taking him to Celtic but didn't follow through with the interest.

That was the type of market we were shopping in. Looking for gems that others hadn't had the patience to work on.

In saying that, there were players who didn't go higher because of their own attitude, and I saw that from the day I started out at Aberdeen through my time at Rangers and at every club I ever played for. You can have all the ability in the world, but you need to want to improve and to make the most of the talent you have. Too many let themselves down.

If I had a weakness as a manager it was probably being too sympathetic when it came to those who couldn't get in the team. For as many good players I signed, I released or sold a lot too because I didn't see the sense in having talented boys kicking their heels on the bench. I'd rather see them go and play elsewhere than have them around our squad just in case we needed them. I always tried to be fair in that respect.

It was a tough division – with the likes of Dunfermline and Falkirk in there – and we laid down a marker with the way we went about it. We were the top scorers in Scottish league football that season, with 82 in 39 games, and all of the pieces of the jigsaw fell into place.

That applied off the park too, where Dennis McCleary was a huge support in his administrative capacity, and the standards were raised and professionalism increased. The ground was improved, commercial income rose, and it was a brilliant time to be around the town and the club.

It was the first time the club had won a championship and that team's still spoken about as the best there's ever been at Berwick, something others are far more qualified to judge than I am.

For me, the league win was a reward for the hard work the players had put in. They deserved it. What more could I ask for as a manager than for them to fulfil their potential? They never let me down.

After promotion we stayed in the First Division at the first time of asking – no mean feat, especially after losing 9-1 in the first match up in that league away to Hamilton. That result didn't change my approach – if we were going to lose we were going to do it playing the way that we felt was right. In the next fixture we went out and beat Hearts. Staying in the division was probably a bigger achievement than winning the championship the year before, and at that stage my managerial stock was high.

We had some big cup ties too in that period – we took Hibs to a replay in the Scottish Cup, drawing 0-0 at Shielfield before falling 1-0 at Easter Road, lost by the only goal of the game to Rangers in the Dryburgh Cup at Ibrox in 1979 as well as the Scottish Cup match at Shielfield that we lost 4-2 the previous year and a 2-0 defeat to Celtic at Parkhead in our title-winning season.

That cup tie against Rangers in 1978 should have grabbed the headlines for all the right reasons but turned out to be front-page news for all the wrong ones, with Willie Waddell and Jock Wallace demanding the tie be switched to Ibrox.

They were citing safety concerns and travelled down to meet with our chairman and the police. Shielfield had all the safety certificates required and we were steadily investing in ground improvements on the back of increased gates.

We were looking forward to welcoming Rangers down and had absolutely no concerns about our ability to host the tie safely. Nobody needed to lecture me about that after everything we had been through with the disaster in 1971. To suggest I would do anything to put Rangers supporters at risk was disrespectful.

To me it felt as though they were trying to use their influence to get an unfair advantage. I don't remember Jock complaining too much about the conditions in 1967 when he was on the other side of the fence and playing for Berwick. Maybe he was worried about lightning striking twice and the result going the wrong way!

Waddell came down to meet with our chairman Jim Reed and police representatives. He was putting pressure on the police to get the match switched, and the SFA were involved too, with the inimitable Ernie Walker right in the middle of it all. Ernie loved a bit of drama and a chance to dust down the rule books, so a high-profile row wasn't a problem for him.

It felt as though Rangers could have handled it better and in a more dignified way. You have to respect the draw. For us, it was a bonus game from a financial perspective, but the focus as far as football was concerned was fully on the league and continuing the good progress we were making.

The game did eventually get played at Shielfield, although Rangers didn't take any tickets in protest, and we gave our reluctant visitors a bit of a scare before they ran out 4-2 winners. Rangers went on to beat Aberdeen in the final, so the little trip south didn't do any harm, and both sets of fans had a great day out – plenty of away supporters still went to the game, despite the club's stance.

James Mortimer, at the height of his empire building in the Glasgow nightclub scene, was one of those I met. He promised me a bottle of champagne for every goal we scored, and he was true to his word. Two big bottles arrived for me after the tie. Maybe if we'd won he wouldn't have been quite as generous!

As an aside, we beat Raith Rovers 6-0 in the previous round and Burntisland Shipyard 4-1 before that to earn the Rangers tie. The long-since retired Bobby Tait was the referee for that game at Burntisland and tells the story of having to reprimand one of their players for trying to hack lumps out of me. Bobby insists he told him, 'You can't go around kicking him, he's a Rangers legend,' or a more colourful version of that. He never did hide his allegiances!

Looking back, there were lots of good times at Berwick. I could have moved on, there were certainly some of the bigger sides who made moves in my direction, but I felt a huge loyalty to the club and the people in the town. Unfortunately, things were changing behind the scenes, and we went our separate ways early the following season.

As odd as it sounds, that championship win with Berwick ranks right up there with Barcelona for me. The two aren't comparable, but they were special in different ways.

I loved my time down there and I hope I gave them plenty to smile about. I've always felt for smaller teams, and by that I mean those that can't sustain full-time football, the aim should be entertainment. That might mean a bit of yo-yoing between the divisions, but for the supporters who follow the likes of Albion Rovers, Berwick Rangers and Stenhousemuir the motivation isn't playing in the Champions League. It's about being part of a community.

That was certainly the case at Berwick, where you got to know just about everyone connected with the club, and they responded to what we were trying to do.

I wanted players to go out with freedom and to express themselves and to play to their strengths. Davie Moyes is a case in point. He was a rough-and-ready player and did a fantastic job for me – that was his strength, and I'm the first to admit it wasn't something I ever could or would do. He would have kicked his granny if it meant Berwick won, but off the park he was a great lad.

I'm still in touch with quite a few of the squad. We ended up living close to Stewart Wheatley in Fife after retiring, where he still runs his garage. Peter Davidson, who has been hugely successful in the motor trade in Newcastle, is another I've stayed in contact with.

Leaving Berwick was a turning point. There were decisions to be made. We'd flitted from Newton Mearns to Dunblane, to South Africa and America then to the Borders in a pretty short period of time. My daughters Amanda and Melanie had shuffled around schools to fit with my career, my son Paul was just three and it was a choice again of following the work and chasing the next contract or putting down roots.

I went back to playing with short spells helping out Meadowbank Thistle and Hamilton, playing alongside a young man by the name of John Brown during that spell, and there was the potential for a longer stint coaching with the Accies. But after a decade away from home in the North-east, we felt it was the right time to get closer to family in and around Aberdeen.

We settled back in the North-east and I had brief spells as player-manager at Huntly and Peterhead before real life kicked in. I spent a long time as a taxi driver in Aberdeen and had a pub in Montrose before retiring, so I can say I know what real work is.

SEVENTEEN

'NOT THE IDEAL PLACE FOR AN UNASHAMED FOOTBALL IDEALIST'

I READ, SEE and hear a lot about football philosophies. From Johan Cruyff and Total Football to Pep Guardiola's Tiki-Taka and Jürgen Klopp's heavy-metal football, there are plenty of different ways to win a game.

My own philosophy is, probably, a big part of the reason I didn't stay in coaching beyond my days as a player-manager. When I was on the park I could set the tone and play a part that was impossible from the sidelines. I never wanted to compromise.

I suppose what I've come to realise is that the hurly-burly of the Scottish game's not the ideal place for an unashamed football idealist.

To try and explain, I'll rewind back to later in life when I was taking my son Paul's boys' club team in the 1990s. There's a careful distinction there already – I don't claim that to be coaching. For me, young players should be free to play and express themselves as much as possible. I was there as the responsible adult, even if it maybe felt the other way round for the boys a lot of the time! Training was a good excuse for me to get the trainers back on and play.

I know that relaxed approach goes against a lot of what you'll find in coaching manuals, but I do feel the way we go about things in this country we've knocked individuality out of young players by over-coaching. Looking from the outside, it seems that rather than one or two outstanding players the clubs want 11 at the same level who can do the same things. Squads are levelled down, not up, with the standout players pulled back to fall in line rather than pushed to excel.

Paul, like me, started as a left-back and as he grew in his teens I always thought he had the potential to be a centre-half in the mould of my big brother Doug.

In truth, I've always said he was too well brought up. Sheila takes all of the praise for the way Amanda, Melanie and Paul were raised. They're a credit to her and the way she dedicated her life to giving them the best life possible. She did everything for them, loves them with all of her heart, and in turn they have made us both incredibly proud.

Banchory, where we lived after I retired from football through to when our three flew the nest, was a wonderful place to raise a family. On Royal Deeside and buoyed by the oil boom that spilled out of Aberdeen and into the surrounding areas, it was as far away from city life as you could get despite being only half an hour away.

It was the first time we had settled anywhere for any length of time, and the friends Paul grew up with there are still as close now as they were when they were at school.

As an aside, growing up as a Rangers supporter in Aberdeenshire brings its own quirks and not least the accusation of being a glory hunter. Paul and his good friend William Totten could always have a laugh to themselves when they got hit with that – both of their dads had been there in Barcelona in '72, with William snr adding his voice in the crowd that night and still attending every game at Ibrox. It was very much in the blood for them both.

That boys' club team in Banchory that I mentioned was different to the teams which we were playing against from just 15 miles down the road in Aberdeen and different again from sides from further afield. They didn't have the same nasty streak.

I remember Jimmy Calderwood, a proud Glasgow boy raised in Castlemilk, arriving in Aberdeen as manager and coming to the conclusion that young players coming through at Pittodrie and in the North-east as a whole didn't have the swagger and the gallous streak he was used too.

In a roundabout way he was saying the same as me – that he was finding players who were just too nice. I don't think Jimmy meant that as a compliment, but believe me when I say that I certainly do.

What sums up my own philosophy, and I don't really like using that word, is the advice I gave to that team and to any young player:

- Don't clear the ball if you can dribble with it instead. Whether in your own six-yard box or pinned in the corner, there's never an excuse for putting it into touch. If you can nutmeg the opponent you're up against, that's worth bonus points.
- If, in the process of dribbling out of your own box, you get fouled then you're too slow.
- Don't head the ball unless you absolutely have to. It's called football for a reason.
- Tackling isn't the mark of a good player. One interception is worth ten tackles in my book, and a defender hammering into challenge after challenge has got something wrong in the first place.
- Keep your kit clean if you can. A player coming off the park covered in mud and blood isn't the mark of a job well done. Stay on your feet.

- No bookings. Doug and I between us turned out in well over 1,000 top-class games as defenders; neither of us had a yellow card against our name. It's brain over brawn for me every time, and if you're counting cards as some sort of badge of honour, you're in the wrong game.
- Don't swear. An 'Oh dear' will do the job!

Of course, the reality is most managers, not all, want the complete opposite. But, and there is a big but, if you get the chance to play with that freedom it can be a lot of fun.

Jumping back to my days as a manager in the Scottish Football League and Highland League, the problem, and it maybe took me too long to realise it, is that it doesn't always bring results and particularly if I wasn't on the pitch to do my bit.

Would I change my approach if I could do it all again? As much as I hate losing, I don't think I could.

Although managing in the lower leagues and non-league was a frustrating place to be at times, we made an awful lot of good memories.

I like to think I made it a good environment to play in, and if you speak to 99 per cent of those who played under me at any level they'll remember games or moments in matches which bring a smile to their face. There's more to football than snarling your way through training sessions and fixtures.

If I've always been quick to give my opinion in football, I've never claimed to be the best person to be handing out life lessons to anyone. I guess if there's is one piece of advice I can give it's that we all take a lot of knocks in life, but it's how you bounce back from them that matters.

I am incredibly proud of our family. Amanda, our eldest and an academic at heart, has had a long career in science at home and abroad, most recently in a lab in Iceland, and now works in the care sector back in Scotland. After graduating from university, Melanie and her husband Pascal lived and worked in Australia and across America, settling in San Diego with their sons Zak and Tom, where they've built a wonderful life. Paul, who worked in and around football for a long spell as a journalist, has had great success as an author alongside his full-time role as a marketing director. He lives in Aberdeenshire with his wife Coral and their children Finlay, Mia and Zara.

Through all the ups and downs in life, we're all still together and there's another generation ready to take on the world. That for me brings a far bigger sense of achievement than any of the medals in the drawer.

Forgive me for getting all sentimental on you – back to football, in a round about way.

There's a team that means as much to me as the Barça Bears and they probably don't know it themselves. The Fraserburgh Rangers Supporters' Club – or, to give it the full title, the Dave Smith Loyal Fraserburgh Supporters' Club – helped me fall in love with football all over again.

I got into the game because I loved everything about playing. When that's taken away from you by old Father Time, it takes an awful lot of adjusting to.

I played junior football into my 40s, but your body tells you when it's time to stop. As much as I felt I could go on forever, deep down I knew the game was up. Not that I ever admitted it or accepted it.

Those post-football years are difficult. I still took Paul to games, whether at Pittodrie or trips to Ibrox and Hampden for Rangers' cup finals, but I'll be brutally honest and admit it's difficult to enjoy watching games which you are pining to be playing in. As odd as it sounds to say it, that sense didn't leave me until I was into my 50s. I'd go to games and get hit with the 'Have you got your boots with you Davie?' quips, all the time wishing I did and feeling like I could still do a job.

The one salvation I had was a weekly game of five-a-sides at the old Linksfield Academy, where the Aberdeen Sports Village stands now. That was the Friday night carrot for the rest of the working week. It was with a great group of boys, some of who had played a bit in the league or Highland League, but there were no airs and graces. It was just about playing and getting back to where it had all started really, kicking a ball about for fun.

One of that five-a-side squad was Dave Hamilton, a Rangers supporter through and through who has become a great friend over the years. Dave travelled with the Fraserburgh bus, and over time I began to join them too, eventually leading to the name change. There's even the Dave Smith bus complete with its personalised licence plate in my honour!

Being part of that team has given me the camaraderie which all supporters' club members will recognise. As resident quiz master, I'd like to think I've given hours of entertainment back – those who have had to suffer those journeys might beg to disagree.

I've been incredibly well looked after by everyone connected with the Fraserburgh club, not least Dave, Ritchie Reid and Billy Paterson. From Ian McLean, Scott Ramage, Kevin Alexander, Kevin Buchan and Alex Buchan to the younger crew who have grown up as part of the club - including Eddie, Johnny and AJ – and many other good friends. It has kept this old man feeling like he's still got some life left in him. We've travelled home and away, in Europe and to the NARSA conventions. We've been through the lower league years, the big Europa League nights and, albeit via Zoom, through to celebrating 55 titles and beyond.

They've listened to me moan about how things were better in the good old days, they've tolerated my terrible jokes.

To me it demonstrated what being part of the Rangers family is all about. I cannot thank them enough for taking me under their wing.

Through the Dave Smith Loyal I'm a season ticket holder,

where you'll find me in my usual seat in the Sandy Jardine Stand. I enjoy being back home at Ibrox as often as I can.

I have Rangers running through my blood. The club has been a massive part of my life and that bond with it, with the supporters, the city and with Ibrox never leaves.

What that doesn't mean is I see everything through blue-tinted glasses, something some in the support maybe haven't always appreciated or maybe don't understand.

I haven't done a huge amount of broadcast work over the years. The occasional radio contribution, in more recent times a handful of podcast guest slots and very rarely some TV. It has never been something I've craved or pursued, but if I'm able to help out I'm happy to.

It was one of those rare forays into television, with Rangers TV, that shone a light on the different way I see the game.

Doing co-commentary with Tom Miller during one of the games on the journey back to happier times, I came in for a bit of stick from fans – and not just for my broadcast skills and dulcet Aberdonian tones.

The biggest bone of contention was my suggestion that some of the players that day weren't Rangers class. Now, I understand that club channels are supposed to be cheerleaders and to talk up the product, but unfortunately that's not in my make-up. Maybe that's why I haven't been asked back!

There's no sense in raking over old ground and naming names. It was never intended to be personal, just an observation based on decades playing the game and many years following Rangers through thick and thin.

What I saw during those seasons coming back up through the leagues was dispiriting. Players who weren't worthy of wearing the shirt and, worse still, some who were going through the motions.

I remember taking my grandson Finlay down for a day out at

Ibrox that was part of a Christmas present, to a Scottish Cup tie against Raith Rovers in 2015. The idea was that we'd go to all of the cup games and maybe, just maybe, end up at Hampden with a glimmer of silverware in the gloom of that period.

Instead, we sat through a dismal 2-1 defeat. The first time Raith had won at Ibrox since before my time as a player, a fifth Rangers defeat in the space of nine games. Some present that turned out to be!

Amid all the lows, and there were plenty at that time, that was painful. It wasn't the Rangers I knew, it wasn't a Rangers team we could be proud of.

Roll forward a few years and we were standing side by side watching the real Rangers matching Villareal in a packed Ibrox. A long road, but worth every step.

My observation about Rangers class came around the time of that display against Raith, which hints at the pace of the rebuilding job. It wasn't levelled at anyone showing a lack of heart, far from it, but solely on ability.

People didn't like to hear it at the time, but how many of the players from the Mark Warburton and Pedro Caixinha eras survived through to 55? Not many. That was the point I was making at that time.

It was clear that the quality wasn't there, not to reach that level and get back on top. That isn't even a criticism of the individuals who did their best but came up short. Rangers class to me is something different, it's another level. Plenty of players that don't hit those heights go on to have great careers elsewhere, and I'd never wish anything less for anyone who crosses that line on a Saturday.

Don't forget I was held up to the same standards as a player. As I recounted, a certain Willie Waddell had pondered in print whether I was Rangers class. Fortunately, he came up with the right answer!

In more recent times, during the climb back through the leagues, too many people were blinded by loyalty to the club and didn't see the reality of the team and players at that time. They pinned their hopes on players who were equipped to deliver physically, mentally or technically. You need all of those qualities to align to be a Rangers player, whereas at other clubs you can perhaps get by with a piece or two of the jigsaw missing.

Maybe the comments I made came across as an old timer harking back to the good old days and seemed out of touch, but I'm relaxed about that. I may have a few extra years under my belt, but I'm still confident in my ability to read a player. The ins and outs at Ibrox on the run to 55 backed up 99 per cent of the calls I've made. There will be a few more to follow if the club wants to keep improving, that's the nature of the game.

I listened to some being proclaimed as superstars after a game or two and was the voice of reason (or is that pessimism!) at the back of the supporters bus, urging caution. Eventually, they ended up with a return ticket or found themselves kicking their heels in the stands.

The team that did deliver 55 did it as a unit and all played their part, but even then I was cautious. The process couldn't end, there were areas of that side that needed to be reinforced and even within the management and coaching team at that time it felt there was a tendency to play to the crowd. The players should always be the focal point, which was far from the case.

It may not always have sounded that way, but all I ever wanted was to see a team on the park that was able to get back on top.

EIGHTEEN

'AS THE YEARS PASS THE REUNIONS BECOME SMALLER'

LOVE YOU, SON. Three words that I'll never forget, and that sum up the bond between us that's so difficult to put into writing.

That was how Sandy Jardine and I said goodbye, for what turned out to be the last time. I'd bumped into him at Ibrox during his cancer treatment, and as we spoke I just had the feeling he knew what lay ahead. Typically of Sandy, there was no fuss or drama, and he was determined to stay positive.

I'm so glad I did use those words when we parted, it's how I felt about him and about all of those who went through the experiences in and around Barcelona together. As gruff old men, we're not always great at telling each other, but there will come a day for all of us when it's too late.

Sandy's passing in 2014 left a huge void in the Rangers family.

The following year we lost Colin Jackson to leukaemia, another great blow to the club.

Sandy was only 65, Colin just 68. Taken far too young, and men who had lived their lives the right way and been supreme athletes. Sandy would spend his summers taking part in sprint meetings — he was a match for the professionals on the games circuit.

Despite what we might think, we're not immortal. Sandy and

Colin's deaths have proved that in such tragic circumstances, and I find it difficult to comprehend that they're not still with us. We had already mourned Andy Penman, who died in 1994, and nothing prepares you for that in such a close-knit group.

When the '72 squad get together it's like we're boys again, as we were then. Don't forget we had a couple of teenagers in our ranks, and for those of us who were a little older – 28 in my case – we still had that feeling of being unstoppable. The world was at our feet and a long winding road ahead of us.

As the years pass the reunions become smaller, a fact of life but it doesn't make it easier to accept. It would have been wonderful if we had made it to the 50th anniversary together, but it makes it all the more important for those of us who are around to represent the squad to make sure we treasure the occasion.

We don't see as much of each other as we should, but when we're together it's as if we've never been apart. We're not strangers, and that's the main thing. It catapults you back 50 years and keeps you feeling young, even if we don't look it. A few more grey hairs, a few less perms.

Peter McCloy was the foundation the team was built upon. A gentle giant off the park, a colossus for us on that run and for so many years after. Of course, I'd argue he was playing behind a defence that made his life an awful lot easier!

Peter was a fine goalkeeper and one of several who didn't get the recognition from outside the club that he deserved, certainly not in terms of international caps.

He arrived at a difficult time, and as a goalkeeper there's no hiding place, but Peter had the perfect nature for one of the toughest assignments in football. Being a keeper for any team, whether it's on a public park or in front of a paying crowd, isn't a job I would thank you for. The margin for error is zero, every decision is crucial. When you take on that role for Rangers it is on another level completely. Peter spent more than a decade and a half at the club, under a succession of managers, and that tells you everything you need to know.

Naturally, his aerial presence was a huge factor and, as a defender, to see him coming and claiming high balls the way he did gave such confidence. He never got ruffled. I can't remember him ever losing his cool, and he always carried himself as a Rangers player should.

That too was the case with Sandy, both during his playing days and just as importantly in the darkest of days for the club. He was there when the vultures were circling, and I hope that he was looking down with that big smile of his when all of that was finally put to bed and 55 was won.

I've spoken about the softer side to Sandy, but he had steel at his core which served him well. As a player he was immaculate, so comfortable on the ball with an athleticism which would have made him just as successful in any era. I think that's what made it so difficult to comprehend when Sandy did pass away – he was so fit and lived his life like the consummate professional he was. It just underlined how indiscriminate cancer is.

Not surprisingly for a player who had started out as an attacker, he had a grace and poise which weren't typical of a Scottish defender. Not that he was confined to stopping the opposition play – there was freedom to get up and down that right side, and he took that at every opportunity.

Sandy was another unflappable character, a bit of a recurring theme as you work through the '72 team. That sense of calm running through the side was a massive part of the success that season, even when the chips were down and pressure was building there was never a sense of losing control or focus.

Sandy broke into the team at around the same time as I had arrived, and it was a pleasure to see his career flourish the way it did over such a long and consistent period. It felt as though he got better and better with every year that passed.

Willie Mathieson, on the opposite flank, was another vital cog in the machine. Like Peter, Willie didn't often get his name up in lights in the way that some did but he never once let the club or his teammates down.

Willie was a selfless player and came into his own in '72, with more freedom to get forward and the defensive ability that he was renowned for. If you wanted a man beside you, it was him – as a friend as well as a colleague. That friendship is worth more to me than anything we achieved on the park.

Willie was a powerful defender, well-built and a nightmare to play against. Much more than that, he was deceptively quick, and I never saw anyone run away from him. That pace provided a real threat going forward too and, like Sandy, he thrived on the opportunity to join in the attacks.

Off the field he was an unassuming character, comfortable in himself and what he was about. We clicked and always got on well. Willie is six months older than me, and John Greig had a couple of months on him, so we were the older heads and the three of us were a good mix. We shared a lot of good times together over the years.

The fact I turned to Willie as my assistant when I took the manager's job at Berwick tells you everything you need to know. In that role you want someone who sees things the same way you do, on and off the pitch, but most importantly you need someone you trust implicitly. He was all of those things.

John was at No. 4 that night, our captain. He was the type who led by example. He never left anything on the pitch and was a tough character, definitely another one you wanted to be with you rather than against. I know – I played against him! It sounds strange to say, given he's been voted the greatest-ever Ranger, but John didn't always get the credit he deserved – he was far more skilful than people appreciated.

I'll always remember marking him in a game at Pittodrie, up

at the Merkland Road end, and he flicked the ball over my head before smashing a volley into the roof of the net. If a Brazilian had done it we would never have heard the end of it. Mind you, I'm not sure John let me forget it either!

He scored a few worldies over the years – the one for Scotland against Italy sticks in the mind – and that's a measure of the ability he had.

I've touched upon the bond we struck up already, rooming together over a long period. As life takes you in different directions those friendships naturally fade over time, but in the build-up to the anniversary there's a sense of togetherness about the group as there was back in '72, and all of us enjoy being back together when we get the opportunity.

John was the only one of that group who went on to manage the club, something every one of us who had ambitions in coaching would have loved ultimately to achieve, and he was dealt a very difficult hand in trying to replicate the success he had enjoyed as a player.

The stature he held and the experience amassed made him the natural choice, but in reality it was a club in transition and facing a very powerful challenge from all sides. The emergence of Aberdeen and Dundee United was a long time in the making, but when it came it only served to make the Rangers job even tougher. I was looking in from the outside during that period but, like everything he did, I know John gave it 100 per cent.

If John, Willie and I were among the old men in Barcelona, at the other end of the scale was Derek Johnstone. At 18 years old you could say he had the fearlessness of youth, but I don't think that attitude changed with age. Nothing fazed Derek – when the biggest of occasions rolled around he just shifted up a gear and motored through it.

Even today he lights up a room when he comes into it, a contrast to us 'Aberdeenies' as he'd be quick to let you know! I don't recall him ever being any different, even as a rookie he had the same sense of fun, and you need that in any group to keep things lively.

Derek's one of a kind, and it was a privilege to be there alongside him at the start of a quite incredible journey.

From scoring the winner in a cup final to picking up European silverware, his first couple of years in the first team were a whirlwind. He must have thought it was always going to be that way, but he knew what it meant to work hard for the success that followed.

He had all the ingredients of an all-round football player – if you were to build an identikit it would be in his image. Fantastic in the air (a godsend for me, given I rarely headed a ball), talented with the ball at his feet and strong in the tackle. Derek could cover a lot of ground too and you knew from that early age that he could be whatever he wanted to be. He was at the heart of some huge moments in time for Rangers and always stepped up when it came to the crunch.

Tommy McLean's time at Ibrox coincided with DJ's, and both were instrumental in so many great victories. Tommy was an intelligent player and a thinker when it came to football, so it was no surprise to see him flourish as a coach and manager.

Given the way his brothers Willie and Jim had taken to that side of the game, it was natural he would follow them into the dugout. Tommy was very much his own man though, and what he went on to deliver for Motherwell in particular was remarkable. He built the team and club with a pragmatism and typical tenacity. What he did always want his players to do was look forward first, and that's something I think a lot of coaches could learn from.

The public tend to see the serious side, but Tam's got a dry sense of humour, and that added to the dynamic of a special group. He could also be led astray by Messrs Greig, Mathieson and Smith on occasion!

To be tasked with replacing Willie Henderson, as he was, tells you everything you need to know about the esteem he was held in by Willie Waddell. A technically gifted and direct player, he took on that responsibility with a real energy.

He was a different player than Willie had been for us, not the same type of mercurial winger. Tommy could certainly beat a man, but he mixed things up and was just as likely to pick a pass as he was to dig out a cross. He was entrusted with a lot of the dead-ball deliveries and that points towards the ability he had.

Alfie Conn, at No. 8 on the night, was another with technical ability – but the key to Alfie's success was his imagination. He loved to play spontaneously and, even at 20 in Barcelona, had the confidence to try things. For all that swagger on the pitch, Alfie was a gem off the park and quieter than his on-field persona suggested.

He was one of the east-coast contingent who travelled across by train each day. We had Sandy Jardine and John Greig from Edinburgh and Colin Stein from Linlithgow, then Alfie along with Willie Johnston and Willie Mathieson based in Fife. To have more than half the team commuting across the country like that you might think it would be a bit cliquey, but it was never like that.

I guess the only downside was it meant nights out weren't a regular occurrence, so the European trips were important in building those bonds.

Alfie deserves the recognition as a Rangers legend for his contribution. The way he is still revered by the Tottenham support underlines the impact he had south of the border after moving on from Ibrox, and there's no doubt he was a special talent.

It was maybe a surprise to some supporters when Alfie got the nod for the final, ahead of some of the more experienced players in the squad who could have come in, but it didn't feel that way for those of us who saw him go about his work every day in training. He'd proven himself, and there wasn't a single person in that squad who would have doubted Alfie's ability to come in and make an impact.

Like Derek, I'm sure he thought occasions like Barcelona would come around every season. He was just starting out on the journey, whereas those of us who had been over the course were viewing it differently.

Colin Stein was *the* Rangers No. 9 in my opinion. Barcelona was the defining moment for Steiny, but he had so many others in a blue shirt. He had everything you could ask for in a striker and a little bit more, the type of instinct that you just can't teach.

He was by no means a giant, but Colin had the knack of playing as though he was 10ft tall – there wasn't a defender in the land who relished going up against him. Colin was bold and brash on the park, a fierce competitor, but he's a man with a big heart and that counts for far more than anything he achieved on the pitch. He looks out for his friends, I know that.

The knack for being in the right place at the right time was a big factor in his goalscoring record, but what the statistics can't show is the amount of work Colin put in for the team. He didn't give defenders a minute's peace, hustling and harrying right across the backline and forcing them into areas they just didn't want to be in. He must have been an absolute nightmare to play against, and any lapse in concentration ended with the ball in the back of the net.

He also suffered for his striking art, taking a lot of big hits. Leaving a mark early was very much part and parcel of football then, as John's challenge on Sabo in Barcelona demonstrated, and nine times out of ten Colin was the one on the receiving end for us. The tackles would fly in, and he just bounced back up, more determined than ever and more than capable of looking after himself.

Alex MacDonald, at No. 10, was the beating heart of that team in so many ways. Doddie's dynamism in midfield drove us all on, and his energy was, and still is, infectious. He was living his dream and it showed in the way he went about his work, with commitment and a real football brain.

How he didn't go on to be a mainstay of the Scotland midfield for a generation is a mystery to me, but the national team's loss was Rangers' gain, and he gave such incredible service to the club over a long and distinguished career.

It's incredible to think he was the only Glasgow boy in the team for the final, and he relished every minute he played in a blue jersey. In saying that, we may not have all been local but to a man we bought into the club and what it meant to the supporters. Once a Ranger, always a Ranger.

Doddie had such a pivotal role to play, literally. He was there right at the heart of the pitch, and he wasn't afraid to graft.

That's another theme that shines through when you sit back and look at the '72 side – from 1 to 11 we were all willing to put in a shift and work for one another. It's pretty unique to get a group like that. There are usually one or two luxury players who you accept you'll have to work around, but we managed to combine both sides of the game.

It was no coincidence that Doddie's teams at Hearts and Airdrie displayed the same type of endeavour that made him a star. He wouldn't have accepted anything less.

Last, but far from least, on the Barcelona team sheet was Willie Johnston. I count myself lucky to have spent a fair bit of time with Bud and Steiny in recent years, maybe a touch of *Last of the Summer Wine* about us as a trio!

As you get older you don't take those friendships for granted, and the biggest compliment I can pay is that neither has changed – Bud's the same happy-go-lucky boy that we all knew and loved. As a player he is so difficult to describe, a world-class talent with the fiery side that made him a dream to play with and a nightmare to come up against. One of the greats of the Scottish game, of that there can be no dispute.

The thing with Bud was that he had the sheer pace to take him away from any defender – he could just knock the ball and go if he wanted to. The great thing was that he didn't like to be predictable – for every time he went past his man there was another when he would leave him on the floor after tying him in knots.

The moment when he sat on the ball in the semi-final against Bayern Munich at Ibrox is the one that's etched in my mind, one picture that sums him up better than a thousand words ever could. I don't think the Bayern players could quite take it in – they paused to watch. That was the cheeky side that we all knew and loved. That wasn't disrespect or anything else you want to call it, just entertainment and value for money.

Like Colin, Bud took a lot of abuse from opposition players. Like Colin, he could take care of himself. It would have been nice if both had been given a bit more protection from the referees, but it didn't stop either from expressing themselves.

Barcelona was about far more than 1 to 11. Those who did play that night can count ourselves lucky, and on the flip side there was a whole group who were incredibly unlucky not to feature.

Injury robbed Ronnie McKinnon and Colin Jackson of the opportunity of a lifetime, two rocks for Rangers and among the best central defenders to have graced the Ibrox pitch. As I've touched upon already, it was a joy to play alongside both, and a pleasure to work with them day in and day out. They both had the physical attributes, including pace, to play that role but had the guile to match.

Watching Ronnie struggling to come back from his leg break was particularly hard for us all. He was a big character, and we were desperate to see him overcome that injury, but it just didn't happen for him. He was the fittest of all of us before being hit with that, as quick over ten yards as he was over 50, 100 or 200. Ronnie looked like he was gliding when he ran, and even in training what was hard for the rest of us was a breeze for him.

The pain for Colin in missing out was offset by the fact he went on to play many more games and win plenty of medals, although I appreciate how big a blow it must have been at the time.

Guile was a quality Willie Henderson and Andy Penman had in abundance too, in attack rather than defence. Willie was out of the picture by the time we made it to Barcelona, and Andy just missed out in the final selection, but both would have graced that big stage.

Willie is quite rightly held up as one of the finest wingers the club and country have ever seen, with that unpredictable edge and tenacity to make and score goals. Andy had wonderful attributes too, although probably flew under the radar as a quieter character. Inside that dressing room we all knew the quality he brought to the table.

Derek Parlane deserves special mention for his key role in the run to the final, stepping in to play in the semi-final against Bayern Munich at Ibrox. Anyone who saw that display could have predicted the impact he would have over a long period of time at Rangers – he slotted in as though he was a veteran.

Jim Denny and Graham Fyfe also made cameos during the earlier rounds, and we had Gerry Neef and Bobby Watson on standby as big Peter's deputies between the sticks. Each and every one of them should rightly lay claim to their part in the success of '72, not only in terms of what they brought on the pitch when called upon but also the positivity on the training ground and behind the scenes.

It was a special time, a special group of men – a real band of brothers.

I've lost track of the number of times I've been asked in interviews who the best player was I played with at Rangers.

I would never answer that because it's an impossible question. Everyone has different attributes, a different character and qualities on and off the park.

Fifty is just a number, but it's an important one, and I think it's an anniversary we have all been looking forward to for a long time now. We've marked the other significant dates over the years, but there's something different about this.

I look back at the pictures from the 25th anniversary and, although we maybe didn't feel it then, we were still young men. Life would have been motoring at 100 miles per hour for us all, and it was just another date in the diary back then, a chance for a meal and a catch-up before we went our separate ways and got on with whatever was around the corner.

The 30th, the 40th, 45th – all were marked in some shape or form, but there's always been that sense that 50 was the one to look forward to.

The fact it coincides with the celebrations of the club's 150th year has a nice symmetry to it, and 2022 is a year which will live long in the memories of the supporters, a chance to reflect on the heritage as well as to look forward. There are a lot of good things happening at the club, and I hope the chance is taken to use this as a springboard to a bright future. The supporters deserve a reward for their loyalty.

For the class of '72 it's an opportunity to slip back into the limelight for another 15 minutes of fame. If the truth be told I think we're all too long in the tooth to crave any of that, any desire for that was left in the 1970s and 1980s where it belonged!

We're in a world of streaming, podcasts and social media now – after the page is turned on this year, I think it's a good time to leave that to the next generation.

For now though, we'll embrace it. For one thing it's nice for the younger members of our families to be able to join in and be part of it. Books, a film, commemorative events and whatever else the year brings will make sure they get at least a bit of a glimpse into what their grandads got up to when they still had a full head of hair!

I don't take being part of the year's events for granted. We'll all take time to remember those who can't be with us to mark the occasion, and that leaves a huge void.

The new club museum will provide a lasting tribute to all of the great successes through the past century and a half. It's an honour for our little slice of such a long and illustrious history to be part of the project, and we all share a great sense of pride in that.

We're also bound by shared experiences that run far deeper than anything we faced on the pitch, and for many of us there is one experience that looms larger in our minds than any celebrations or good times we enjoyed.

For me it's important the final words are dedicated to remembering those who did not make it to Barcelona, the 66 who didn't return home to their families and loved ones on 2 January 1971.

Of the team who played against Celtic that day, eight of us also played in the European final the following year. Myself, Sandy Jardine, Willie Mathieson, John Greig, Derek Johnstone, Alfie Conn, Colin Stein and Willie Johnston had that unwanted distinction, but there were many others in the squad during that run – including Ronnie McKinnon, Colin Jackson, Gerry Neef and Willie Henderson – who shared the experiences.

We talk about bravery and courage on a football field. About pressure and about pain. Nothing that happens on the pitch compares to the pain that those families went through and, while we celebrate the memories of the good times, nobody in the Rangers family will ever forget the 66.

Barcelona and '72 was and forever will be dedicated to them.

INDEX

ABOUT THE AUTHORS

DAVE SMITH is a Rangers Hall of Fame member, former Scotland international and recipient of the Scottish Football Writers' Player of the Year award. Victory in the 1972 European Cup Winners' Cup final ensured legendary status at Ibrox for the Aberdonian, who launched his career with his hometown club in the early 1960s before making the move to Glasgow.

PAUL SMITH is an established non-fiction author, with 18 titles for a range of publishers including Birlinn, Black and White, Mainstream and Pitch. A former journalist, including more than eight years as a sports-writer in North-east Scotland and nationally, he has worked in media and corporate communications for more than 25 years.